FIRST
PICTURE
ATLAS

T0014237

Written by Deborah Chancellor

Illustrated by Anthony Lewis

KINGFISHER
LONDON & NEW YORK

KINGFISHER
LONDON & NEW YORK

Copyright © Macmillan Publishers
International Ltd 2005, 2022
This edition published in 2020 by Kingfisher
120 Broadway, New York, NY 10271
Kingfisher is an imprint of Macmillan
Children's Books, London
All rights reserved.

Distributed in the U.S. and Canada by
Macmillan,120 Broadway, New York, NY 10271

Library of Congress Cataloging-in-Publication
data has been applied for.

ISBN: 978-0-7534-7632-1 (HC)
      978-0-7534-7878-3 (PB)

Illustrations by Antony Lewis
Cover Design by Laura Hall

Kingfisher books are available for special
promotions and premiums. For details contact:
Special Markets Department, Macmillan, 120
Broadway, New York, NY 10271

For more information please visit
www.kingfisherbooks.com

Printed in Thailand
9 8 7 6 5 4 3 2 1
1TR/0919/RRD/UG/128MA

EU representative: 1st Floor, The Liffey Trust
Centre,117-126 Sheriff Street Upper,
Dublin 1 D01 YC43

FSC
www.fsc.org
MIX
Paper | Supporting
responsible forestry
FSC® C116313

CREDITS
The Publisher would like to thank the following for permission
to reproduce their material. Every care has been taken to trace
copyright holders. However, if there have been unintentional
omissions or failure to trace copyright holders, we apologise and will,
if informed, endeavour to make corrections in any future edition.

4 Aquatic Images/Shutterstock; 5 Harvepino/Shutterstock;
4-5 Wetzkaz Graphics/Shutterstock; 7 Paulo Henrique Vilella/
Shutterstock; 13 Rob Crandall/Shutterstock; 16 John de la Bastide/
Shutterstock; 19 Ammit Jack/Shutterstock; 22 WDG Photo/
Shutterstock; 24 Anita Ben/Shutterstock; 27 Nostalgia for Infinity/
Shutterstock; 28 Vera Lebedinskaya/Shutterstock; 31 CasyaldoStuido/
iStock; 32 omers/Shutterstock; 35 Dan Breckwoldt/Shutterstock; 37
Andrew Linscott/Alamy Stock Photo; 38 Terri A1/Shutterstock;
41 Alberto Loyo/Shutterstock; 42 Lysogor Roman/Shutterstock; 43
TravelStrategy/Shutterstock

CONTENTS

ABOUT EARTH

Earth is a planet in space. It is shaped like a ball and is covered with land and water. Photographs can show us what Earth looks like. Maps help us understand more about the world.

Countries of the world

A country (such as Italy, map above) is a part of the world with its own people and laws. There are around 200 countries in the world. The number changes if countries break up or join together in new ways.

Continents

A continent is a huge area of land. Some continents, such as South America (map above), contain many different countries. On maps of continents lines are drawn to show the borders between countries. You cannot see these lines on a photograph, because they are not really there.

WHAT IS A MAP?

A map is a picture of Earth that shows natural and human-made features. A globe is a type of map that is made in the shape of a ball, just like Earth itself. We cannot see the whole world at once on a globe. If we want to do this, we need to look at a flat map.

Making a map

To make a flat map, the globe is split into segments, and "peeled" like an orange.

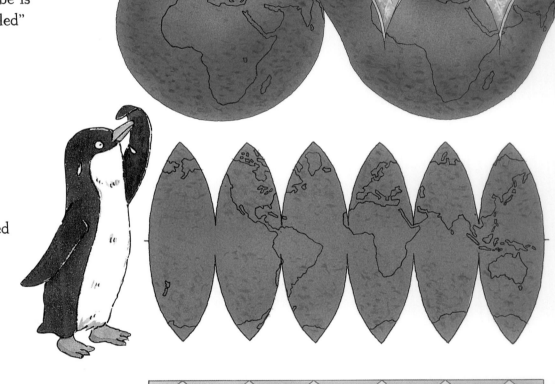

The segments are then placed side by side.

These segments are used to create a flat map (see the map of the world on page 10).

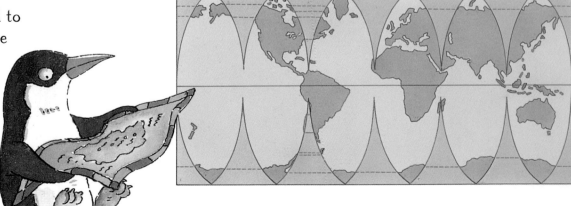

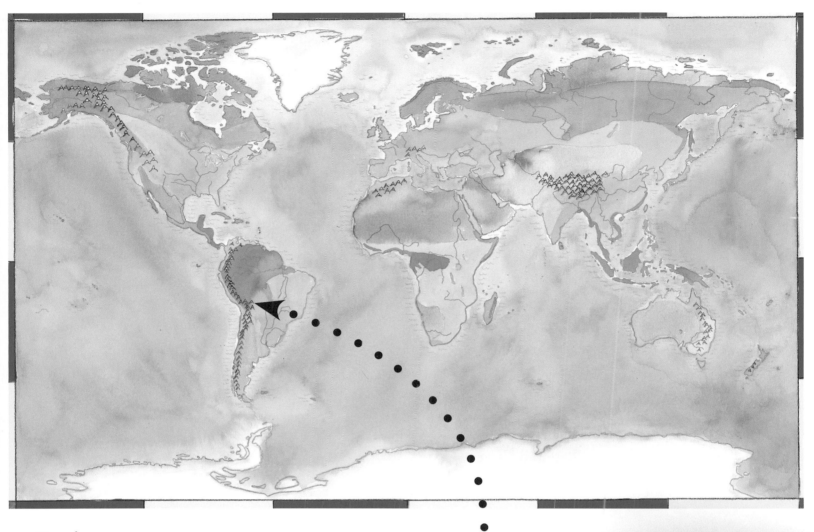

On the map

Most maps show the curved surface of Earth on a flat piece of paper. Mapmakers have to change the shape of some countries and oceans to fit them together on a flat map.

Showing mountains

Special colors and symbols on maps show us where to find important features of the landscape—such as these beautiful mountains in South America.

USING AN ATLAS

An atlas is a book of maps. To use an atlas, you need to understand how maps work. Maps are much smaller than the places they show. They have lots of information in a very small space.

Pictures show industries, animals, or landmarks.

Grid band "C"

A small world map shows you where to find the countries shown on the main map.

Grid band "2"

A grid helps you find places on the map. Here, Alice Springs is in square C2. You can find this by tracing your finger down from the letter C band and across from the number 2 band.

In this atlas, a story box focuses on an interesting fact.

Seahorses

Darwin

Gulf of Carpentaria

Aboriginal cave paintings

NORTHERN TERRITORY

AUSTRALIA

Great Sandy Desert

TROPIC OF CAPRICORN

Mining

Gibson Desert

WESTERN AUSTRALIA

Alice Springs

Simpson Desert

SOUTH AUSTRALIA

Lake Eyre

Kangaroos

The Ghan

Great Victoria Desert

Perth

Farming

Adelaide

Great Australian Bight

Grapes

Great white sharks

Uluru is a sandstone monolith rising high above the desert in Australia's Northern Territory. It is the largest rock of its kind in the world.

Look for the star ✸

Map key

Colors, lines, and symbols on maps stand for many different things. These details are explained in a key to the map. In this atlas, the key helps you find cities, borders, and rivers. It also shows what the colors on the map mean.

KEY

- ■ capital city
- ● city
- • town
- ▲ highest point
- ⌒ country border
- - - - state border
- ···· disputed border
- river
- lake

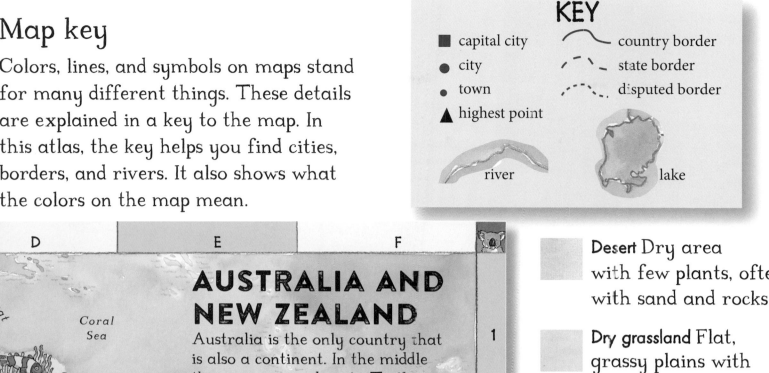

AUSTRALIA AND NEW ZEALAND

Australia is the only country that is also a continent. In the middle there are many deserts. To the north are tropical rain forests. Most Australian people live in cities by the sea. New Zealand is 620 miles from Australia. It is a land of mountains and glaciers. Like Australia, it has many sheep and cattle farms.

Coral Sea

Clown fish

Great ...er

...ng Range

...ENSLAND
...d platypuses

Brisbane

SOUTH ...ALES

Sydney Opera House

Sydney

Canberra
AUSTRALIAN CAPITAL TERRITORY

Surfing

...trait

Tasmanian devils

Tasman Sea

Hobart
...ANIA

Red snapper fish

Fishing

1000km

500 miles

NEW ZEALAND

Kiwi birds

Mount Cook

Rugby

NORTH ISLAND

Auckland
Hamilton

Lake Taupo

Wellington

SOUTH ISLAND

Southern Alps

Christchurch

Dunedin

Yellow-fin fish

Pacific Ocean

39

Desert Dry area with few plants, often with sand and rocks

Dry grassland Flat, grassy plains with only a few trees

Temperate grassland Flat, grassy plains with some trees

Forest Ares with many trees

Mountains Tall hills and rugged land

Tundra Flat area close to the Arctic with frozen ground and no trees

Ice and snow Place where ice and snow cover the ground

Seas and oceans Salty water that covers most of Earth

A scale bar helps you understand how big areas are on the map.

9

NORTH
AMERICA

Atlantic Ocean

*Pacific
Ocean*

SOUTH
AMERICA

*Atlantic
Ocean*

THE WORLD

Maps of the world show the
seven continents. All of the
continents, except Antarctica
and Australia, are made up of
many different countries. Lines
are drawn on world maps that
do not exist on the ground, for
example the equator and the
Tropics of Cancer and Capricorn.

*PRIME
MERIDIAN*

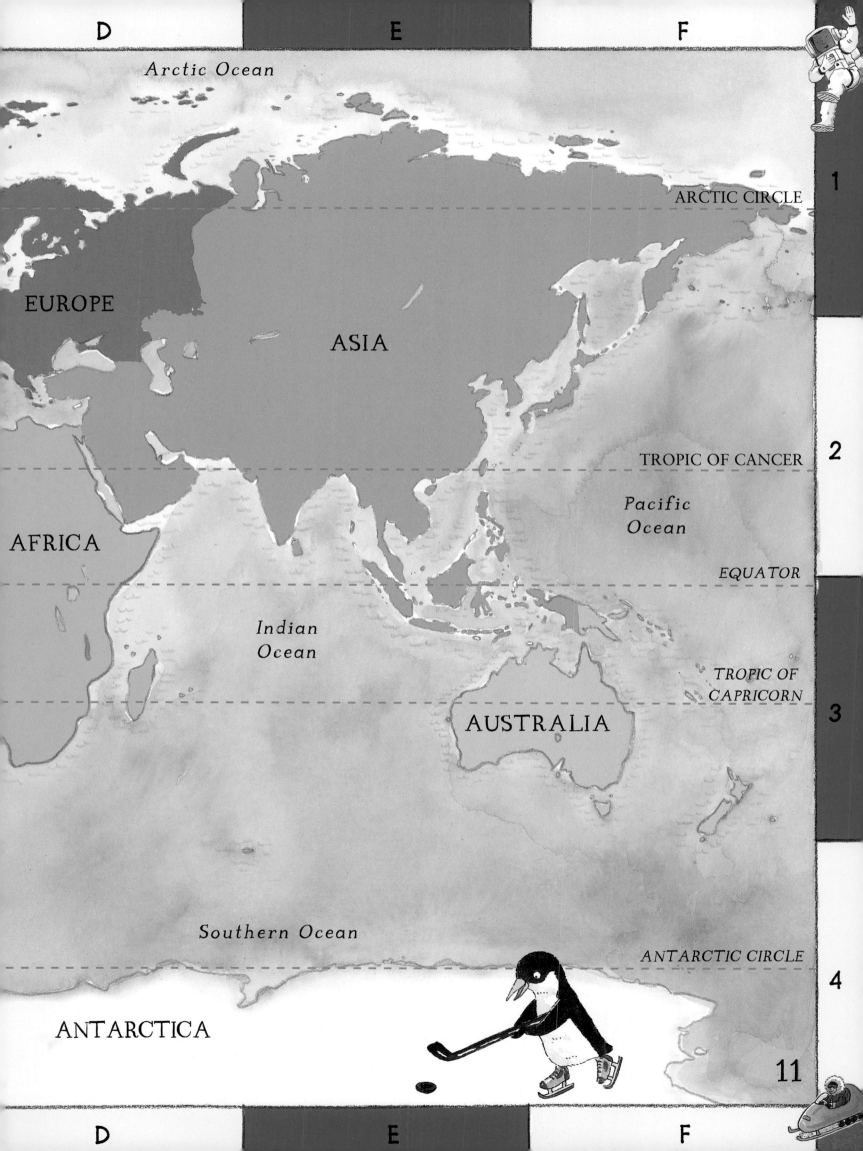

Arctic Ocean

1

ARCTIC CIRCLE

EUROPE

ASIA

2

TROPIC OF CANCER

Pacific
Ocean

AFRICA

EQUATOR

Indian
Ocean

TROPIC OF
CAPRICORN

3

AUSTRALIA

Southern Ocean

ANTARCTIC CIRCLE

4

ANTARCTICA

11

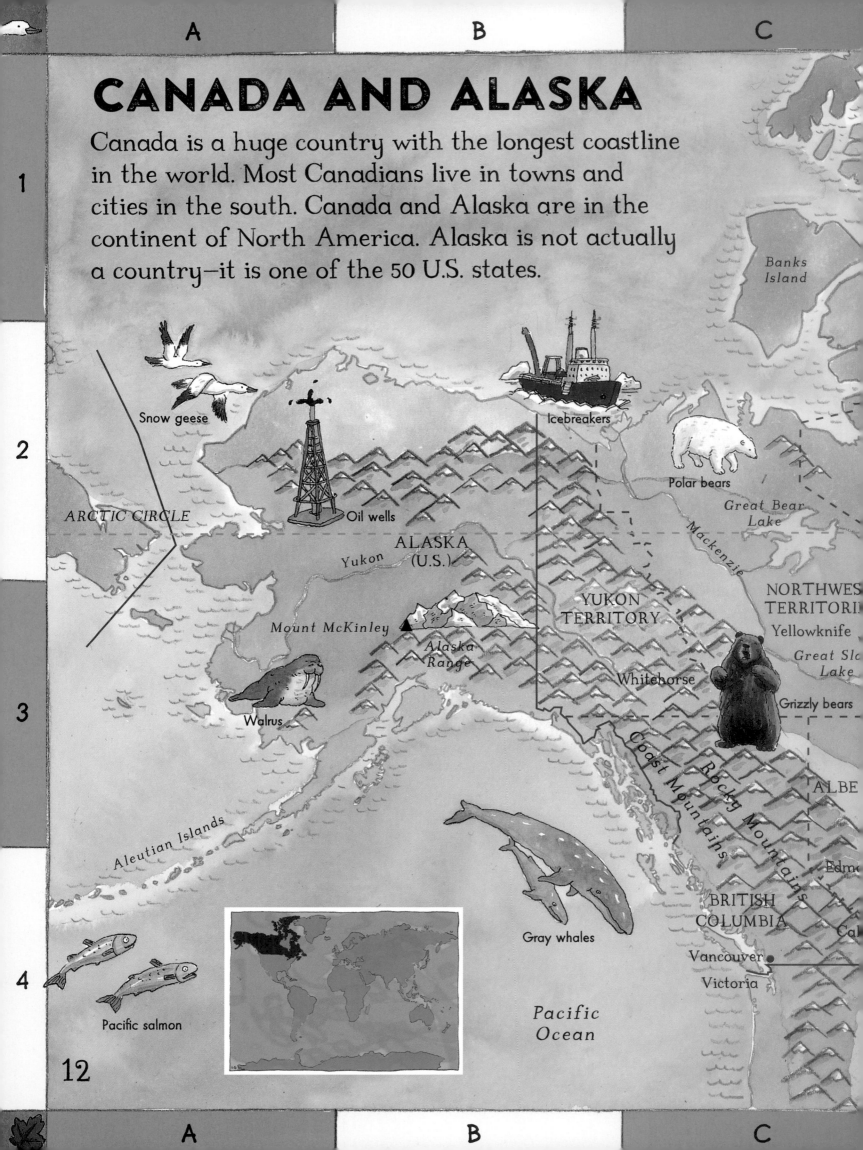

1

2

3

4

CANADA AND ALASKA

Canada is a huge country with the longest coastline in the world. Most Canadians live in towns and cities in the south. Canada and Alaska are in the continent of North America. Alaska is not actually a country—it is one of the 50 U.S. states.

Snow geese

Oil wells

Icebreakers

Banks Island

ARCTIC CIRCLE

Polar bears

Great Bear Lake

Mackenzie

ALASKA (U.S.)

Yukon

Mount McKinley ▲

Alaska Range

YUKON TERRITORY

NORTHWES TERRITORI

Yellowknife

Great Sl Lake

Whitehorse

Walrus

Grizzly bears

Coast Mountains

Rocky Mountains

ALBE

Aleutian Islands

Gray whales

BRITISH COLUMBIA

Edmo

Cal

Vancouver •

Victoria

Pacific salmon

Pacific Ocean

12

1

Queen Elizabeth
Islands

Ellesmere
Island

Devon
Island

Québec is the only
walled city in North
America. It was founded
in 1603 and is almost 400
years old.

Look for the star ✸

Victoria
Island

Baffin
Island

2

NUNAVUT

ARCTIC CIRCLE

Reindeer

Inuit
people

Lake
Athabasca

Hudson
Bay

Icebergs

3

Atlantic
Ocean

MANITOBA

SASKATCHEWAN

Skiing

CANADA

NEWFOUNDLAND
AND LABRADOR

Lake
Winnippeg

Timber industry

QUEBEC

Farming
Regina

Winnipeg

ONTARIO

St
Lawrence

Lake
Superior

CN Tower

Manufacturing

NEW BRUNSWICK

St John's

4

1000km

Lake
Huron

Québec

Charlottetown

Montreal

Fredericton

PRINCE EDWARD
ISLAND

500 miles

Lake
Michigan

Toronto

Ottawa

Lake Ontario

Halifax

NOVA SCOTIA

13

Lake Erie

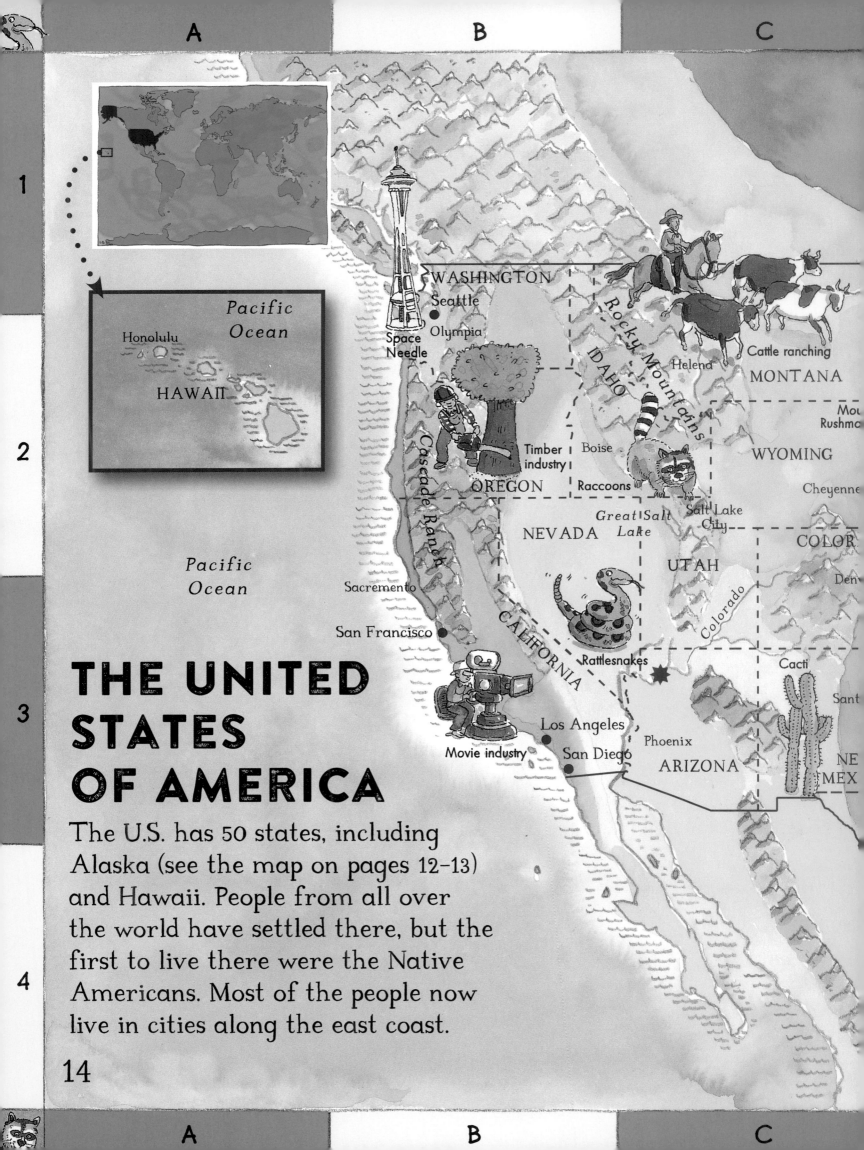

Pacific
Ocean

Honolulu

HAWAII

Pacific
Ocean

WASHINGTON

Seattle

Olympia

Space
Needle

Cascade Range

OREGON

Timber
industry

Rocky Mountains

IDAHO

Boise

Helena

Cattle ranching

MONTANA

Raccoons

WYOMING

Mou
Rushma

Cheyenne

Great Salt
Lake

NEVADA

Salt Lake
City

UTAH

COLOR

Den

Colorado

Sacremento

San Francisco

Rattlesnakes

Cacti

Sant

THE UNITED STATES OF AMERICA

The U.S. has 50 states, including
Alaska (see the map on pages 12–13)
and Hawaii. People from all over
the world have settled there, but the
first to live there were the Native
Americans. Most of the people now
live in cities along the east coast.

Movie industry

Los Angeles

San Diego

Phoenix

ARIZONA

CALIFORNIA

NE
MEX

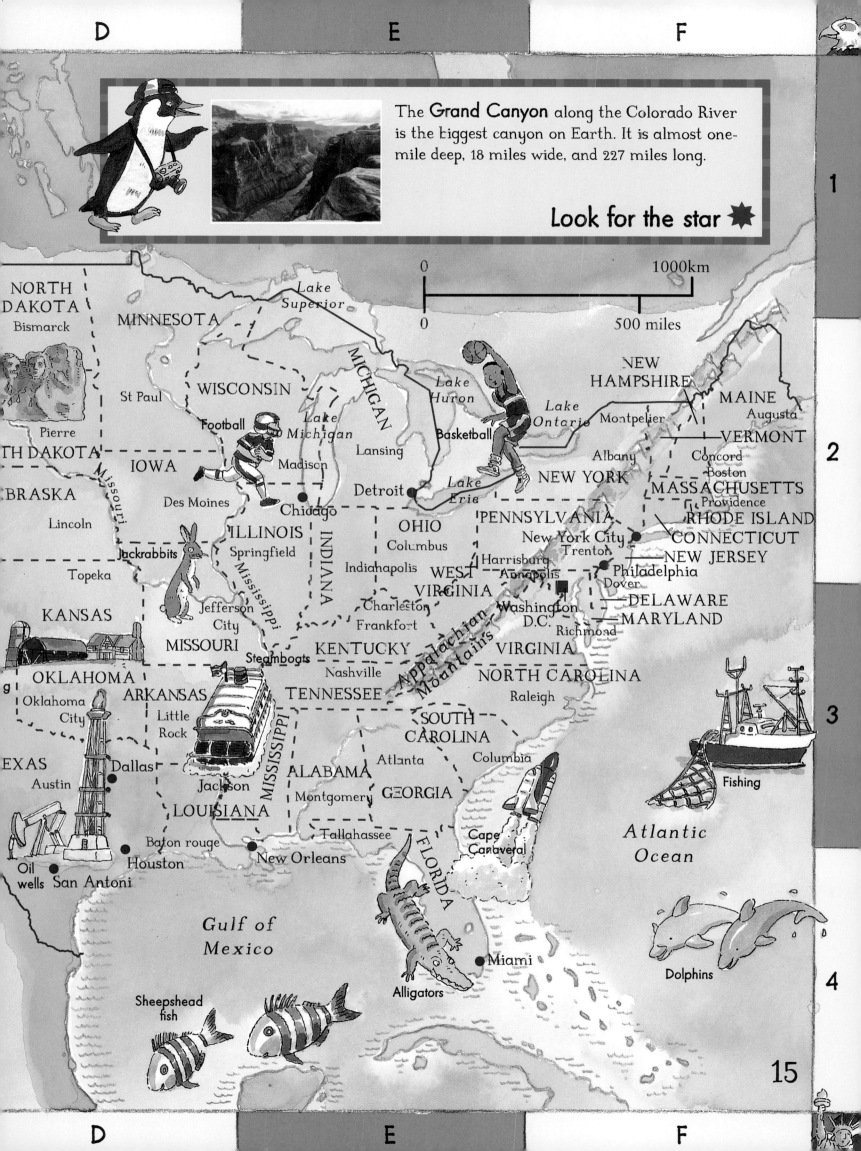

The **Grand Canyon** along the Colorado River is the biggest canyon on Earth. It is almost one-mile deep, 18 miles wide, and 227 miles long.

Look for the star ✷

0   1000km

0   500 miles

NORTH DAKOTA
Bismarck

MINNESOTA

Lake Superior

Pierre

TH DAKOTA

IOWA

St Paul

WISCONSIN

Football

Lake Michigan

MICHIGAN

Madison

Lansing

Lake Huron

Basketball

Lake Ontario

Montpelier

NEW HAMPSHIRE

MAINE
Augusta

VERMONT

Albany

Concord
Boston

BRASKA
Lincoln

Des Moines

Chicago

Detroit

Lake Erie

NEW YORK

MASSACHUSETTS
Providence

RHODE ISLAND

ILLINOIS
Springfield

INDIANA

OHIO
Columbus

PENNSYLVANIA

New York City

CONNECTICUT

NEW JERSEY

Jackrabbits

Indianapolis

Harrisburg

Trenton

Philadelphia

Topeka

Jefferson City

Mississippi

WEST VIRGINIA

Annapolis
Dover

DELAWARE

KANSAS

MISSOURI

Charleston
Frankfort

Washington D.C.

Richmond

MARYLAND

KENTUCKY

Steamboats

VIRGINIA

g

OKLAHOMA
Oklahoma City

ARKANSAS
Little Rock

Nashville

TENNESSEE

Appalachian Mountains

NORTH CAROLINA
Raleigh

EXAS
Austin

Dallas

Jackson

MISSISSIPPI

ALABAMA
Montgomery

SOUTH CAROLINA
Columbia

Atlanta

GEORGIA

Fishing

Oil wells

San Antoni

Houston

LOUISIANA
Baton rouge

New Orleans

Tallahassee

Cape Canaveral

Atlantic Ocean

Gulf of Mexico

FLORIDA

Miami

Dolphins

Alligators

Sheepshead fish

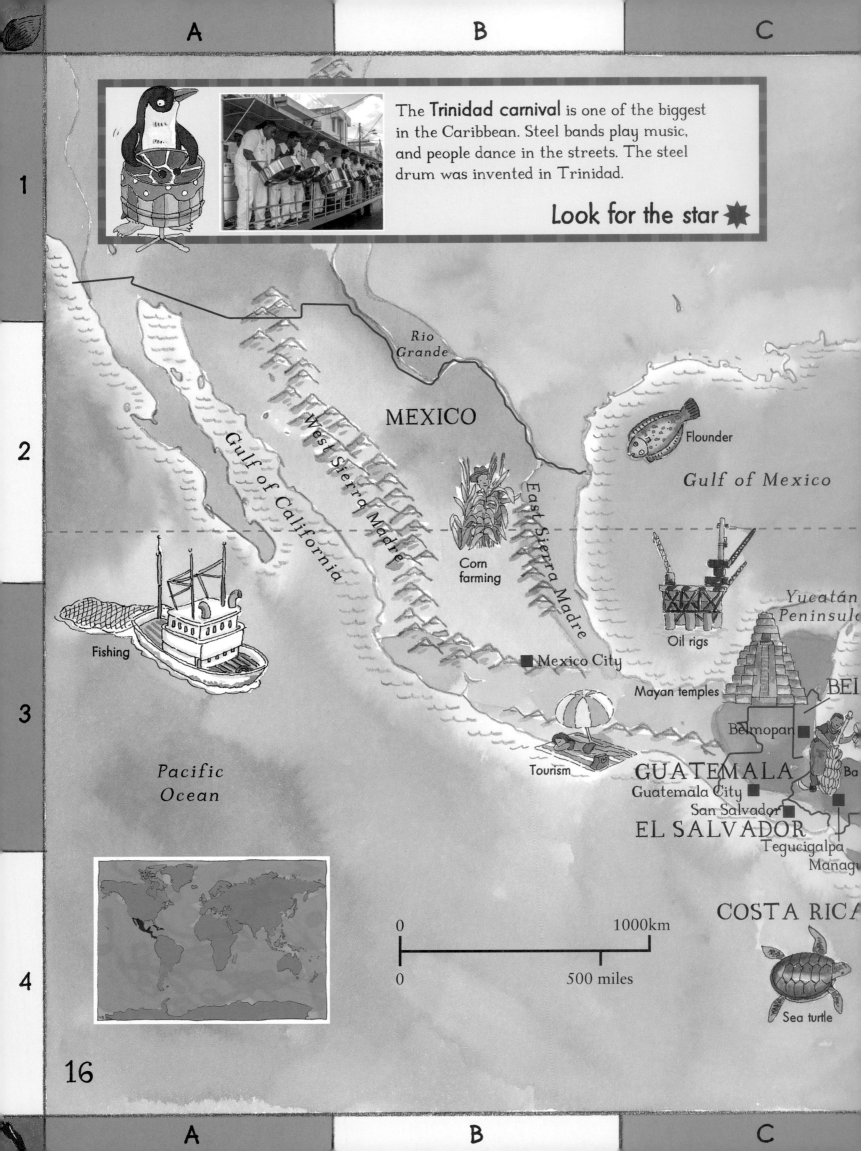

The **Trinidad carnival** is one of the biggest in the Caribbean. Steel bands play music, and people dance in the streets. The steel drum was invented in Trinidad.

Look for the star ✸

Rio Grande

MEXICO

Gulf of California

West Sierra Madre

East Sierra Madre

Corn farming

Flounder

Gulf of Mexico

Yucatán Peninsula

Oil rigs

Fishing

Pacific Ocean

Mexico City

Mayan temples

BEI

Belmopan

Tourism

GUATEMALA

Guatemala City

San Salvador

EL SALVADOR

Tegucigalpa

Managu

Ba

COSTA RICA

0   1000km

0   500 miles

Sea turtle

A   B   C

1

MEXICO, CENTRAL AMERICA, AND THE CARIBBEAN

Mexico, Central America, and the Caribbean islands are in the continent of North America. Mexico is the largest country in the region. The islands of the Caribbean are countries, too. More than half of all Caribbean people live in Cuba and the Dominican Republic.

2

Palm trees

BAHAMAS

■ Nassau

TROPIC OF CANCER

■ Havana

Coral reefs

Scuba diving

Atlantic Ocean

CUBA

DOMINICAN REPUBLIC

HAITI

Sugar cane

PUERTO RICO (U.S.)

■ San Juan

JAMAICA

Kingston

Port-au-Prince

Santo Domingo

ST KITTS & NEVIS

ANTIGUA & BARBUDA

3

DOMINICA

ST LUCIA

ST VINCENT & THE GRENADINES

NDURAS

ARAGUA

Caribbean Sea

BARBADOS

GRENADA

★

Spotfin butterfly fish

■ Port-of-Spain

TRINIDAD & TOBAGO

José

Panama Canal

Panama City

ANAMA

4

17

Caribbean Sea

D   C   B   A

1

EQUATOR

Marlins

Angel Falls

Lake
Maracaibo

Caracas ■

VENEZUELA

Guiana
Highlands

Georgetown ■

GUYANA

Paramaribo ■

SURINAM

Cayenne ■

FRENCH
GUIANA
(FRANCE)

COLOMBIA

Bogotá ■

Quito ■

ECUADOR

Coffee

PERU

Amazon

Amazon
Basin

Blue morpho
butterflies

Toucans

Rain forests

2

Llamas

Machu
Picchu

Lake
Titicaca

La Paz ■

BOLIVIA

Andes Mountains

Lima ■

Atacama
Desert

BRAZIL

Brazilian Highlands

Salvador ●

Brasília ■

Soccer

Christ the
Redeemer
statue

Rio de Janeiro ●

São Paulo ●

TROPIC OF CAPRICORN

PARAGUAY

Asunción ■

Condors

Pacific
Ocean

Rays

3

18

SOUTH AMERICA

South America is a continent of extremes. Tall, snowy mountains lie to the west, while the steamy Amazon rain forest covers a huge area to the north. The southern tip of the continent is very dry and freezing cold.

Airplanes

URUGUAY
■ Montevideo

ARGENTINA
■ Buenos Aires

A Santa Fe

Sheep farming

Oil rigs

■ Stanley
FALKLAND ISLANDS (U.K.)

Patagonia

Cape Horn

Santiago ●
CHILE
Concepción ●

Andes Mount

■

Grapes

Fishing

Sardines

1000km
500 miles
0
0

The Amazon rain forest contains about half of all the animal and plant species in the world. Many are still waiting to be discovered.

Look for the star

NORTHERN EUROPE

Forests, lakes, and mountains cover large parts of northern Europe. The countries Norway, Sweden, and Denmark make up a region called Scandinavia. To the east is Finland. South of the Baltic Sea are the small countries of Estonia, Latvia, and Lithuania.

ARCTIC CIRCLE

ICELAND

Geysers

■ Reykjavik

Iceland cat sharks

Cod

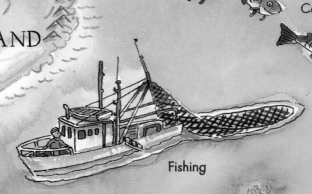

Fishing

Atlantic Ocean

Nor Se

Hans Christian Andersen, a famous children's book writer, lived in Denmark. A statue of his "Little Mermaid" is in Copenhagen, the capital city of Denmark.

Look for the star ✹

20

PRIME MERIDIAN 0°

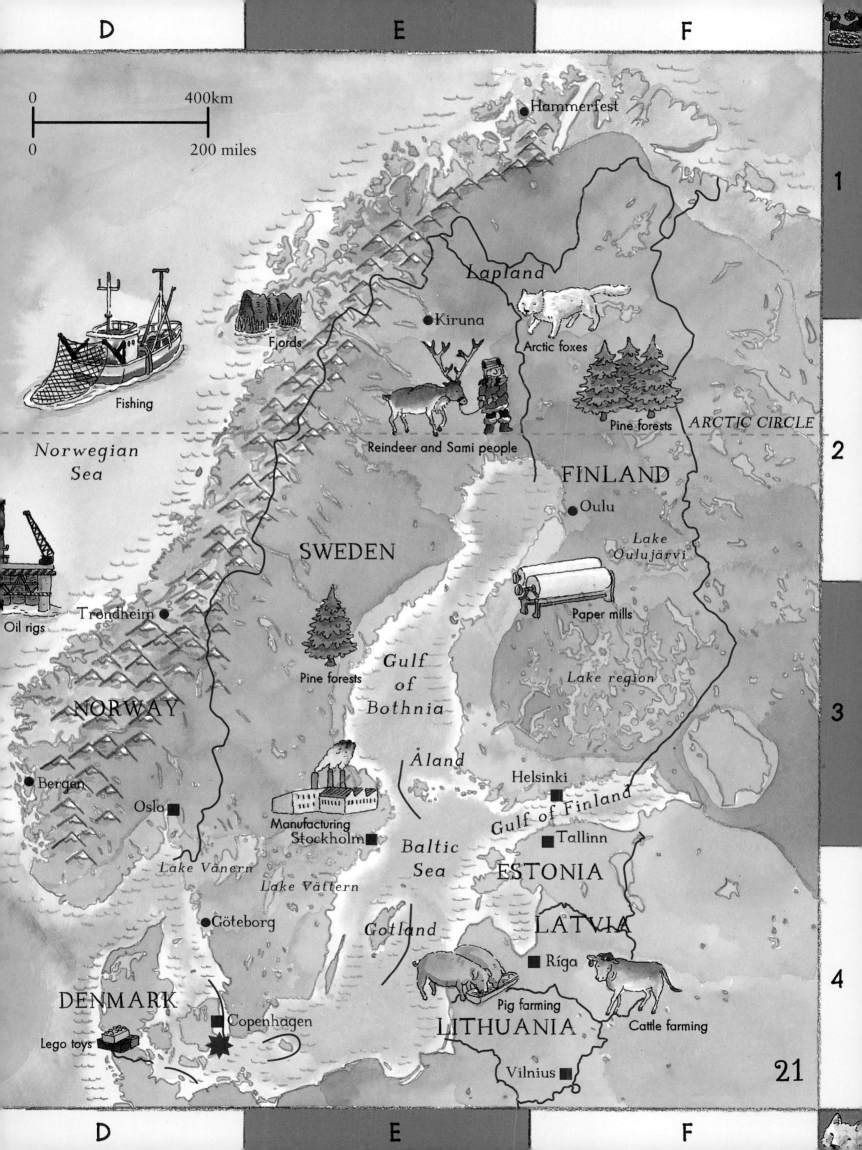

0   400km

0   200 miles

Hammerfest

Lapland

*Norwegian
Sea*

Fiords

●Kiruna

Arctic foxes

Reindeer and Sami people

Pine forests

ARCTIC CIRCLE

FINLAND

Fishing

Oil rigs

Trondheim ●

●Oulu

*Lake
Oulujärvi*

Paper mills

SWEDEN

Pine forests

*Gulf
of
Bothnia*

Lake region

NORWAY

● Bergen

Oslo ■

Manufacturing

Åland

Helsinki
■

Gulf of Finland

Tallinn
■

Stockholm ■

*Baltic
Sea*

ESTONIA

Lake Vänern

Lake Vättern

● Göteborg

Gotland

LATVIA

Rīga
■

DENMARK

Copenhagen
■

Pig farming

Cattle farming

Lego toys

LITHUANIA

Vilnius ■

21

1

2

3

4

WESTERN EUROPE

Much of the land in western Europe is used for farming. Industries, such as car factories, are also important. Some cities are very old and attract many tourists. Countries around the Mediterranean Sea are very hot in summer.

France's most famous landmark, the **Eiffel Tower**, sways up to five inches from side to side in high winds.

Look for the star

Atlantic Ocean

Cod

Puffin

SCOTLAND

Edinburgh

UNITED KINGDOM

NORTHERN IRELAND

Belfast

Dublin

Computers

ENGLAND

Oil rigs

North Sea

Windmills

NETHERLANDS

Tulips

Car factories

Baltic Sea

PORTUGAL

SPAIN

Lisbon ■

Tourism

GIBRALTAR (U.K.)

Madrid ■

Puerta de Alcalá

Pyrenees

Ebro

ANDORRA

Barcelona ●

Sagrada Familia

BALEARIC ISLANDS (SPAIN)

Luxury yacht

PRIME MERIDIAN 0°

400km

0

250 miles

0

FRANCE

Stonehenge

Loire

Grapes

Seine

Paris ■

Tour de France bicycle race

Lyon

Rhône

Marseille ●

Aircraft industry

A380

LUXEMBOURG

Luxembourg ■

Brussels ■

BELGIUM

Soccer

Munich ●

Vaduz ■

LIECHTENSTEIN

Bern ■

SWITZERLAND

Alps

Skiing

MONACO

CORSICA (FRANCE)

SARDINIA (ITALY)

Vienna ■

AUSTRIA

Rhine

SAN MARINO

Po

Ferrari cars

Colosseum

Rome ●

ITALY

Octopus

SICILY (ITALY)

MALTA ■ Valletta

Mediterranean Sea

23

4

5

6

A

B

C

D

In Kazanlak, Bulgaria, **roses** are an important crop. Valuable oil is taken from their petals to make perfume. As many as 60 roses are needed to produce just one drop of oil.

Look for the star

Baltic Sea

Shipbuilding

Gdansk

Great European Plain

Vistula

Warsaw

Coal mining

Krakow

POLAND

Oder

Statue of King Wenceslas

Prague

CZECH REPUBLIC

Danube

Bratislava

SLOVAKIA

St Stephen's Basilica

Budapest

HUNGARY

Lake Balaton

SLOVENIA

Industrial barges

Carpathian Mountains

Grapes

ROMANIA

Farming

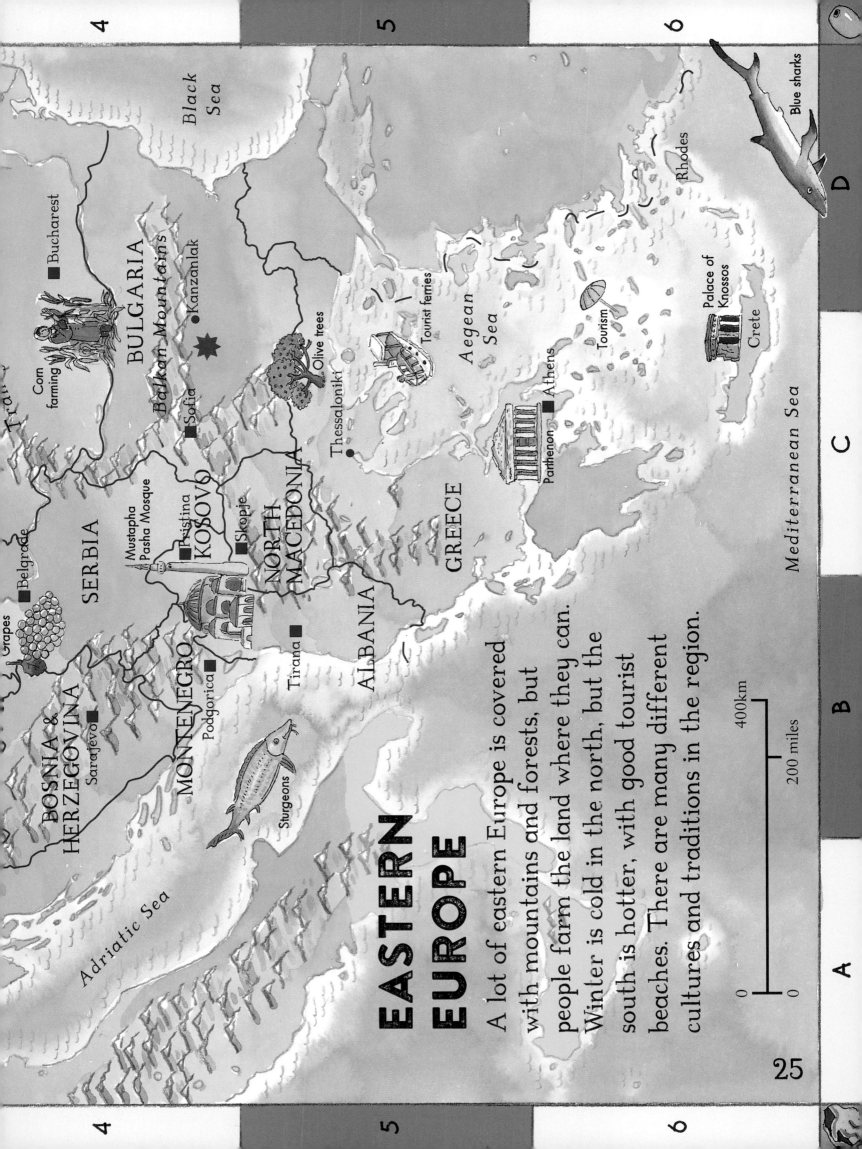

EASTERN EUROPE

A lot of eastern Europe is covered with mountains and forests, but people farm the land where they can. Winter is cold in the north, but the south is hotter, with good tourist beaches. There are many different cultures and traditions in the region.

BOSNIA & HERZEGOVINA
- Sarajevo

Grapes

Belgrade

SERBIA

MONTENEGRO
- Podgorica

Mustapha Pasha Mosque

- Pristina
KOSOVO

- Skopje

NORTH MACEDONIA

- Tirana

ALBANIA

Sturgeons

Adriatic Sea

GREECE

Thessaloniki

Olive trees

Parthenon
- Athens

Tourist ferries

Tourism

Aegean Sea

Crete

Palace of Knossos

Mediterranean Sea

Italy

Corn farming

Bucharest

BULGARIA

Balkan Mountains

- Sofia
- Kanzanlak

Black Sea

Rhodes

Blue sharks

400km
200 miles
0

A B C D

RUSSIA AND ITS NEIGHBORS

Russia is the biggest country in the world. It stretches across the two continents of Europe and Asia. Only one fourth of Russia's land is in Europe, but eight out of ten Russians live in this part of the country. Many languages are spoken in Russia.

Severnay Zemlya

Novaya Zemlya

Polar bears

Murmansk

ARCTIC CIRCLE

R U S S I A

Ural Mountains

Oil wells

Ob

Yenisey

Winter Palace

St Petersburg

Bolshoi ballet

Moscow

Nizhniy Novgorod

Yekaterinburg

Omsk

Novosibirsk

Minsk

Samara

Ural

Nur-Sultan

Manufacturing

BELARUS

Soccer

Volga

Kiev

UKRAINE

KAZAKHSTAN

Oil well

Chisinau

Caucasus Mountains

Caspian Sea

Wheat farming

Aral Sea

MOLDOVA

Black Sea

▲ *Mount Elbrus*

UZBEKISTAN

Bishkek

GEORGIA

Tbilisi

Tashkent

KYRGYZSTAN

ARMENIA

Yerevan

Baku

TURKMENISTAN

TAJIKISTAN

Ashgabat

Dushanbe

AZERBAIJAN

26

The **Baikonur cosmodrome** in Kazakhstan is the world's biggest spaceport. Many rockets are launched from there.

Look for the star ✹

New Siberian Islands

Taymyr Peninsula

Polar cod

Walrus

Pine forests

Lena

S i b e r i a

East Siberian Uplands

Gold mining

Diamond mining

Yakutsk

Kamchatka Peninsula

Tigers

Fishing

Sea of Okhotsk

Seals

ke Baikal

Trans-Siberian Railroad

Amur

Vladivostok

Pacific Ocean

1000km
500 miles

27

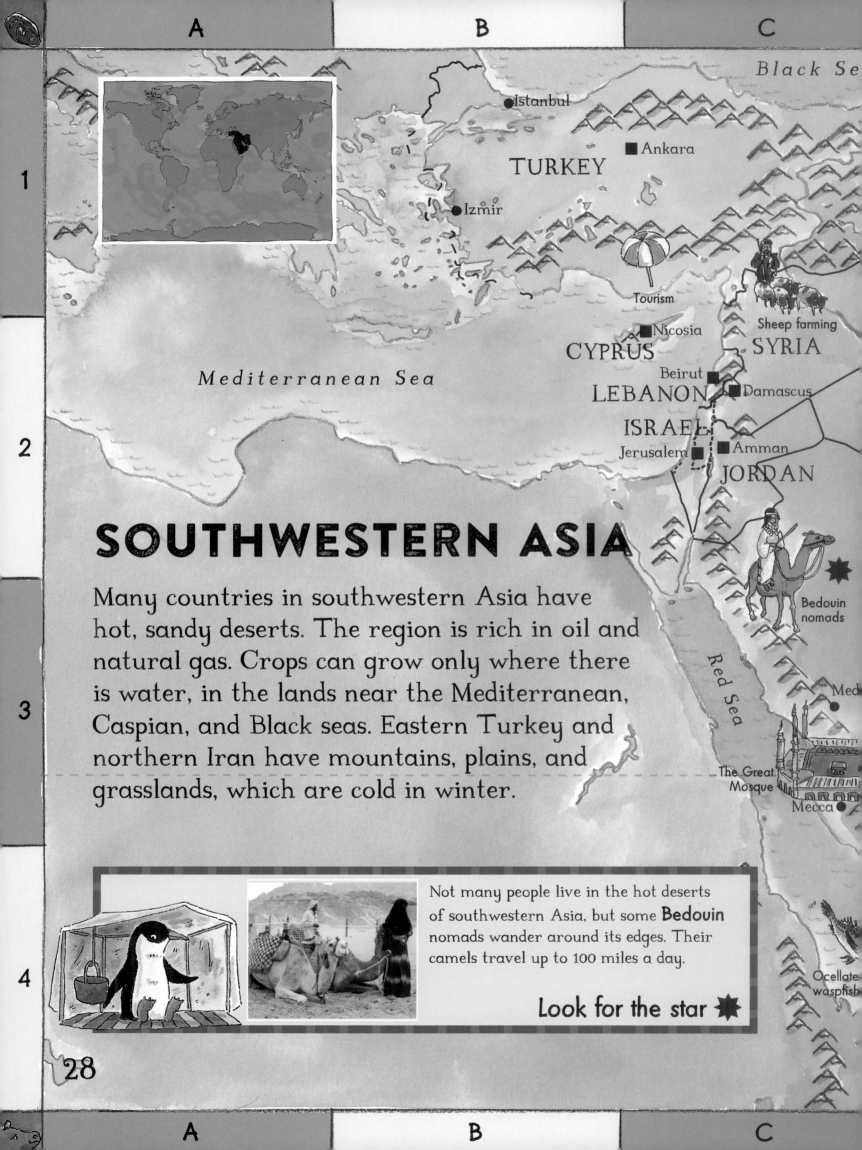

1

Black Se

Istanbul

Ankara

TURKEY

Izmir

Tourism

Nicosia

CYPRUS

Sheep farming

SYRIA

Beirut

LEBANON   Damascus

Mediterranean Sea

ISRAEL

Jerusalem   Amman

JORDAN

2

Bedouin nomads

SOUTHWESTERN ASIA

Many countries in southwestern Asia have hot, sandy deserts. The region is rich in oil and natural gas. Crops can grow only where there is water, in the lands near the Mediterranean, Caspian, and Black seas. Eastern Turkey and northern Iran have mountains, plains, and grasslands, which are cold in winter.

3

Red Sea

Med

The Great Mosque

Mecca

Not many people live in the hot deserts of southwestern Asia, but some **Bedouin** nomads wander around its edges. Their camels travel up to 100 miles a day.

Look for the star ✦

4

Ocellate waspfish

0   800km

0   500 miles

Caspian Sea

Tabriz

Oil rigs

Mashhad

osul

Tigris

Onagers

Carpet making

IRAN

Tehran

Baghdad

Esfahan

IRAQ

Zagros Mountains

Basra

KUWAIT

Kuwait City

The Gulf

Oil wells

Oil refineries

SAUDI ARABIA

BAHRAIN

Manama

OMAN

Oil wells

QATAR

Doha

Riyadh

Abu Dhabi

United Arab Emirates

Muscat

TROPIC OF CANCER

Arabian Desert

OMAN

Dhows

Ar Rub' al Khali (Empty Quarter)

Arabian Sea

YEMEN

Arabian oryx

Orangespotted trevallies

Sana

Dates

Aden

Gulf of Aden

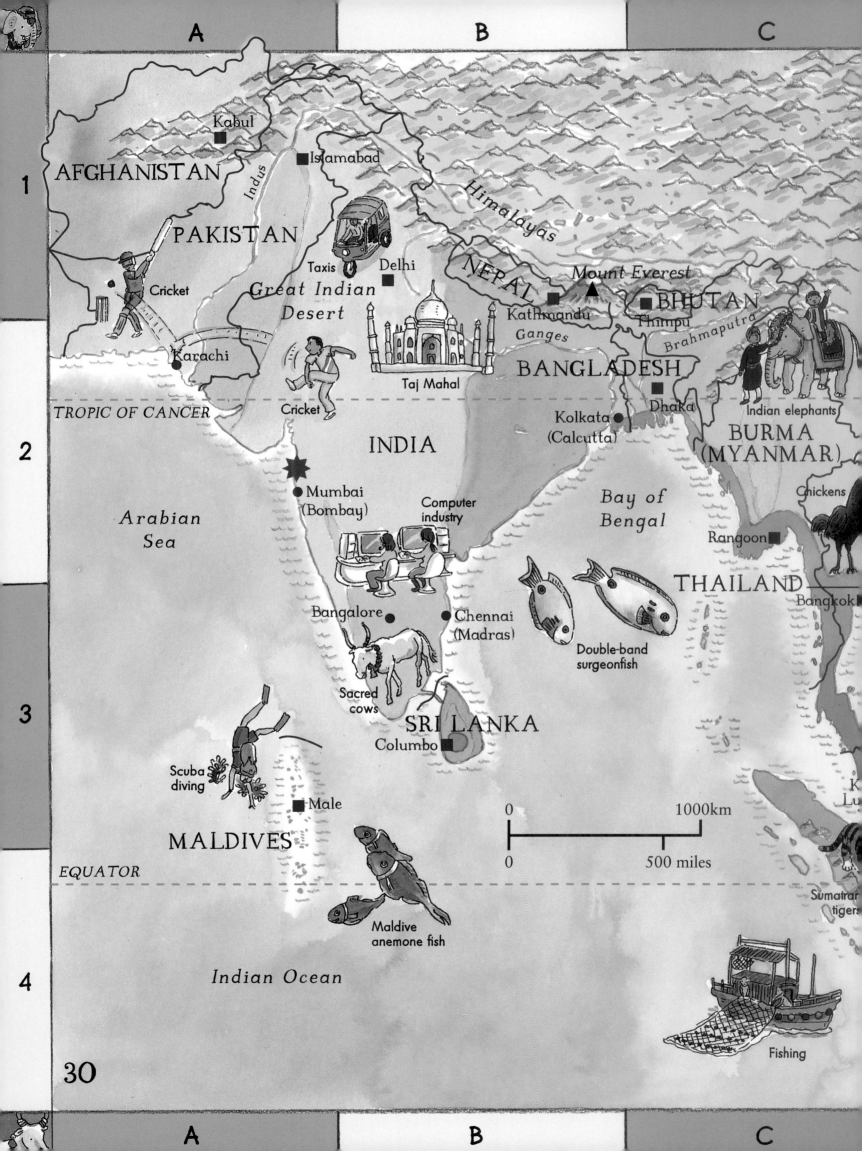

A   B   C

1

Kabul

AFGHANISTAN

Islamabad

PAKISTAN

Indus

Taxis

Delhi

Great Indian Desert

Cricket

Karachi

Taj Mahal

Himalayas

NEPAL

Kathmandu

Ganges

Mount Everest ▲

Thimpu

BHUTAN

Brahmaputra

Indian elephants

BANGLADESH

Dhaka

TROPIC OF CANCER

Cricket

2

INDIA

Kolkata (Calcutta)

Arabian Sea

Mumbai (Bombay)

Computer industry

Bay of Bengal

BURMA (MYANMAR)

Chickens

Rangoon

THAILAND

Bangkok

Bangalore

Chennai (Madras)

Double-band surgeonfish

3

Sacred cows

SRI LANKA

Columbo

Scuba diving

K Lu

Male

0   1000km

MALDIVES

0   500 miles

EQUATOR

Sumatran tigers

Maldive anemone fish

4

Indian Ocean

Fishing

30

A   B   C

SOUTHERN AND SOUTHEASTERN ASIA

The countries of this region are near the equator, so the weather is very hot. Dusty plains stretch across India. Thick rain forests grow in Malaysia and Indonesia. Most people farm in small villages or work in big cities. A long mountain range called the Himalayas lies to the north.

The world's biggest movie industry, **Bollywood**, is based in Mumbai (Bombay), India. About 800 new films are made there every year.

Look for the star ✸

TNAM
■ Hanoi
LAOS
Vientiane

South China Sea

Basket boats

MBODIA
Rice

nom enh

Oil rigs

■ Manila

PHILIPPINES

BRUNEI
Begawan Seri

LAYSIA

INGAPORE
ingapore

Orangutans

INDONESIA

■ Jakarta

Rain forests

■ Dili
EAST TIMOR

31

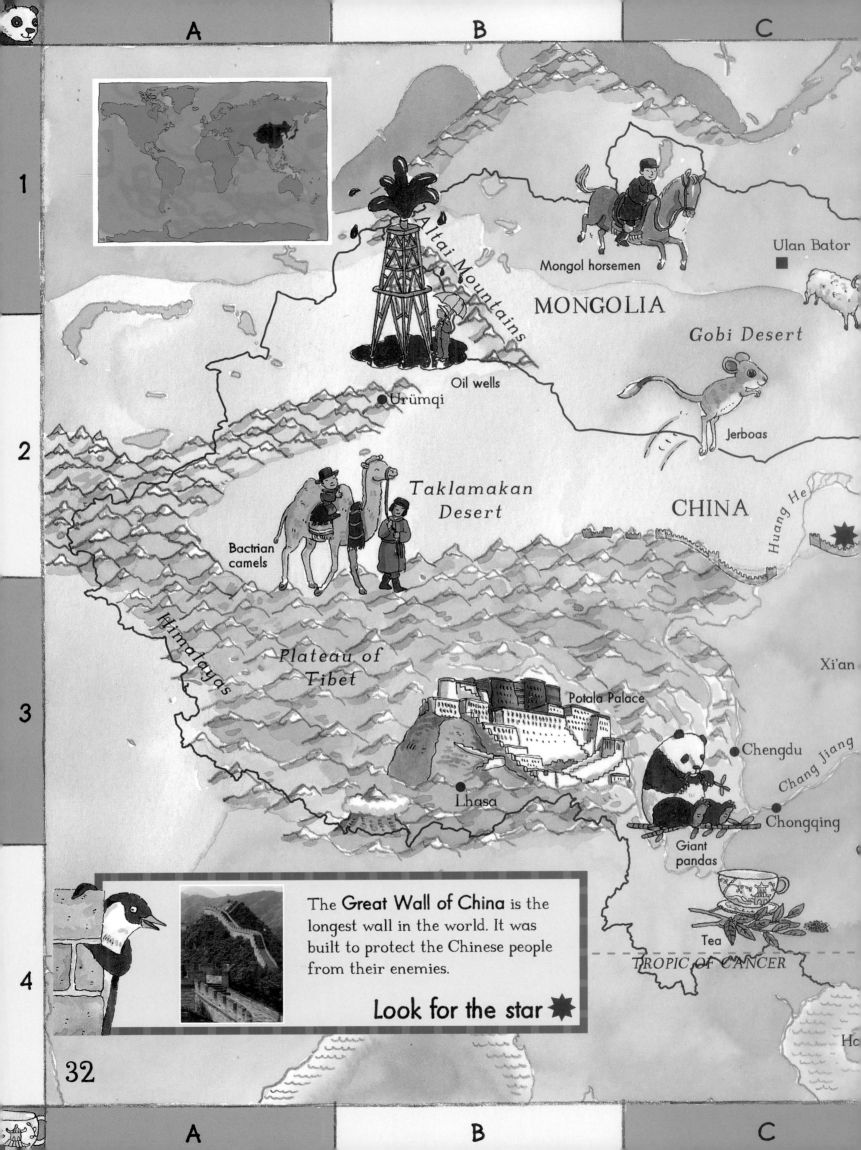

1

Altai Mountains

Mongol horsemen

Ulan Bator

MONGOLIA

Gobi Desert

Oil wells

Urümqi

Jerboas

2

Bactrian
camels

*Taklamakan
Desert*

CHINA

Huang He

*Plateau of
Tibet*

Himalayas

Potala Palace

Xi'an

3

Chengdu

Chang Jiang

Lhasa

Giant
pandas

Chongqing

The **Great Wall of China** is the
longest wall in the world. It was
built to protect the Chinese people
from their enemies.

Look for the star ✹

Tea

TROPIC OF CANCER

4

32

Ha

0   1000km

0   500 miles

1

Great Khingan Range

Sheep farming

Harbin   Manufacturing

The Forbidden City

Shenyang

Hokkaido

Squid

2

NORTH KOREA

Sea of Japan / East Sea

Honshu

Beijing

Tianjin

Pyongyang

Seoul

Skinkansen (Japanese bullet train)

JAPAN

Bulguksa Temple

Mount Fuji

Tokyo

SOUTH KOREA

Himej Castle

Nagoya

Terra-Cotta Army

Osaka

Chinese junk

Shikoku

Wuhan   Shanghai

East China Sea

Kyushu

3

CHINA AND JAPAN

Rice

Taipei

TAIWAN

Guangzhou

Hong Kong

outh China Sea

More people live in China than anywhere else on Earth. Most settle in the east, where they can farm the land or work in cities. To the north is Mongolia, and to the east are North and South Korea, Taiwan, and Japan. Japan is made up of many islands. Most Japanese people live on the four main islands, Hokkaido, Honshu, Shikoku, and Kyushu, in very crowded cities.

4

33

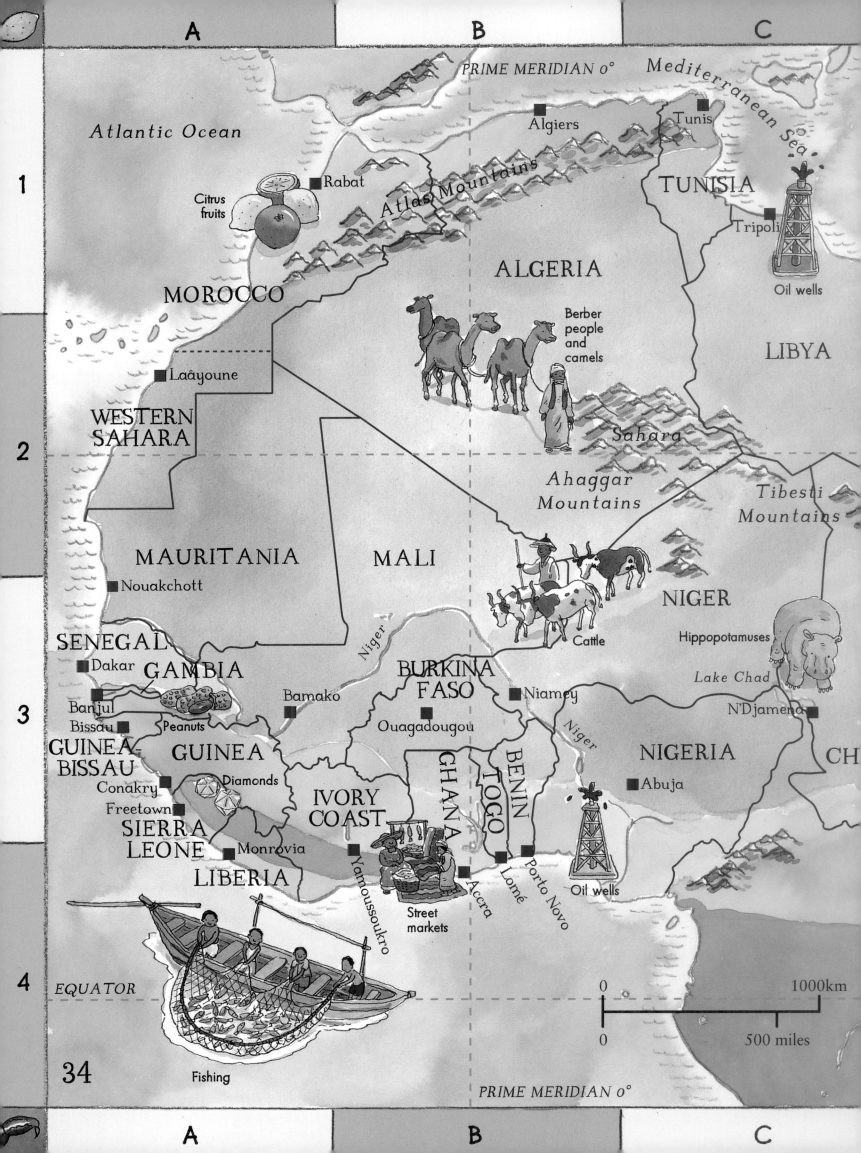

1

Atlantic Ocean

PRIME MERIDIAN 0°

Mediterranean Sea

Algiers

Tunis

TUNISIA

Citrus fruits

Rabat

Atlas Mountains

Tripoli

Oil wells

MOROCCO

ALGERIA

LIBYA

Berber people and camels

2

Laâyoune

WESTERN SAHARA

Sahara

Ahaggar Mountains

Tibesti Mountains

MAURITANIA

MALI

Nouakchott

NIGER

Niger

Cattle

Hippopotamuses

Lake Chad

3

SENEGAL

Dakar

GAMBIA

Banjul

Bissau

Peanuts

Bamako

BURKINA FASO

Ouagadougou

Niamey

N'Djamena

GUINEA-BISSAU

GUINEA

Conakry

Diamonds

NIGERIA

Abuja

CH

Freetown

IVORY COAST

GHANA

TOGO

BENIN

SIERRA LEONE

Monrovia

Yamoussoukro

Accra

Lomé

Porto Novo

Oil wells

LIBERIA

Street markets

4

EQUATOR

0   1000km

0   500 miles

34

Fishing

PRIME MERIDIAN 0°

NORTHERN AFRICA

The Sahara is the world's biggest desert. It stretches across the all of northern Africa. Most people live south of the Sahara or near the coast. The world's longest river, the Nile, flows from central Africa, through Egypt to the Mediterranean Sea.

TROPIC OF CANCER

1

2

Scorpions

EGYPT

Tutankhamun's funerary mask

Cairo

Red Sea

Lake Nasser

SUDAN

Cotton

Nile

Khartoum

Crocodiles

Asmara

Ethiopian Highlands

DJIBOUTI

3

Addis Ababa

SOUTH SUDAN

Juba

ETHIOPIA

SOMALIA

Mogadishu

Starry triggerfish

4

The **pyramids**, near Cairo in Egypt, were built more than 4,000 years ago. They are the largest stone buildings in the world.

Look for the star ✦

Indian Ocean

35

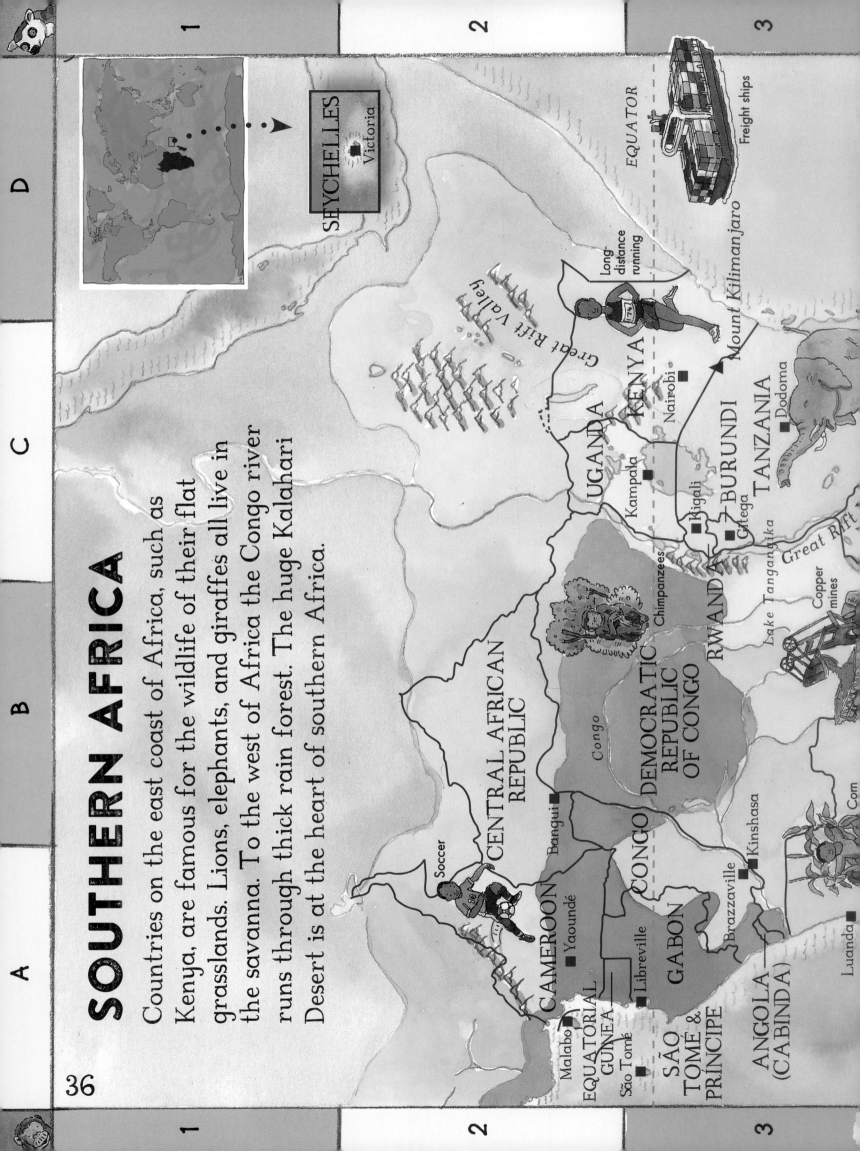

SOUTHERN AFRICA

Countries on the east coast of Africa, such as Kenya, are famous for the wildlife of their flat grasslands. Lions, elephants, and giraffes all live in the savanna. To the west of Africa the Congo river runs through thick rain forest. The huge Kalahari Desert is at the heart of southern Africa.

SEYCHELLES
Victoria

EQUATOR

Freight ships

Mount Kilimanjaro

Long-distance running

Great Rift Valley

KENYA
Nairobi

UGANDA
Kampala

RWANDA
Kigali

BURUNDI
Gitega

TANZANIA
Dodoma

Lake Tanganyika

Great Rift

Copper mines

Chimpanzees

CENTRAL AFRICAN REPUBLIC

Bangui

Congo

DEMOCRATIC REPUBLIC OF CONGO

CONGO

Soccer

CAMEROON
Yaoundé

Libreville

GABON

Brazzaville

Kinshasa

EQUATORIAL GUINEA
Malabo

São Tomé

SÃO TOMÉ & PRÍNCIPE

ANGOLA (CABINDA)

Luanda

Con

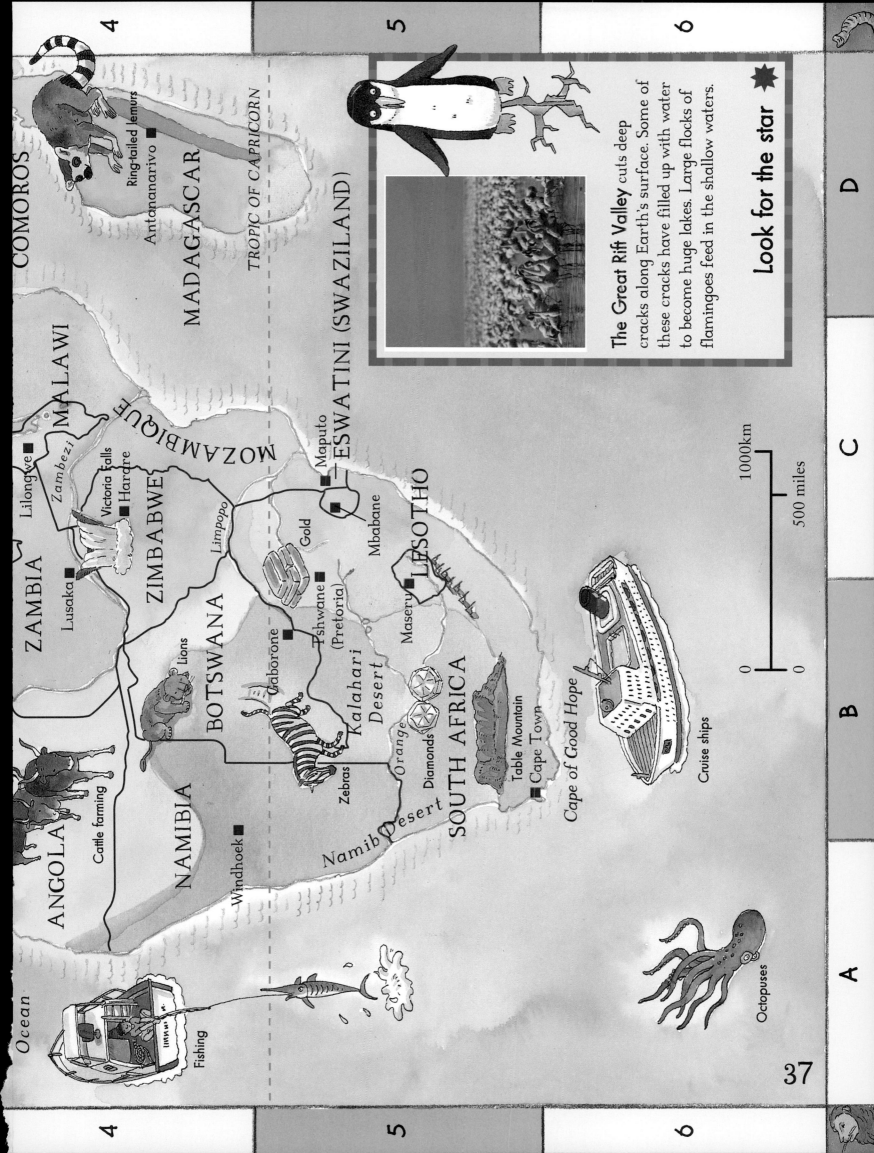

COMOROS

Ring-tailed lemurs
Antananarivo

MADAGASCAR

TROPIC OF CAPRICORN

ESWATINI (SWAZILAND)

Look for the star

The Great Rift Valley cuts deep cracks along Earth's surface. Some of these cracks have filled up with water to become huge lakes. Large flocks of flamingoes feed in the shallow waters.

MALAWI
Lilongve
Zambezi
MOZAMBIQUE
Victoria Falls
Harare
ZIMBABWE
Maputo
ZAMBIA
Lusaka
Limpopo
LESOTHO
Gold
Mbabane
Tshwane (Pretoria)
Maseru

1000km
500 miles
0 0

ANGOLA
Cattle farming
NAMIBIA
Windhoek
BOTSWANA
Gaborone
Lions
Kalahari Desert
Zebras
Orange
Diamonds
SOUTH AFRICA
Table Mountain
Cape Town
Cape of Good Hope
Cruise ships

Namib Desert

Ocean

Fishing

Octopuses

37

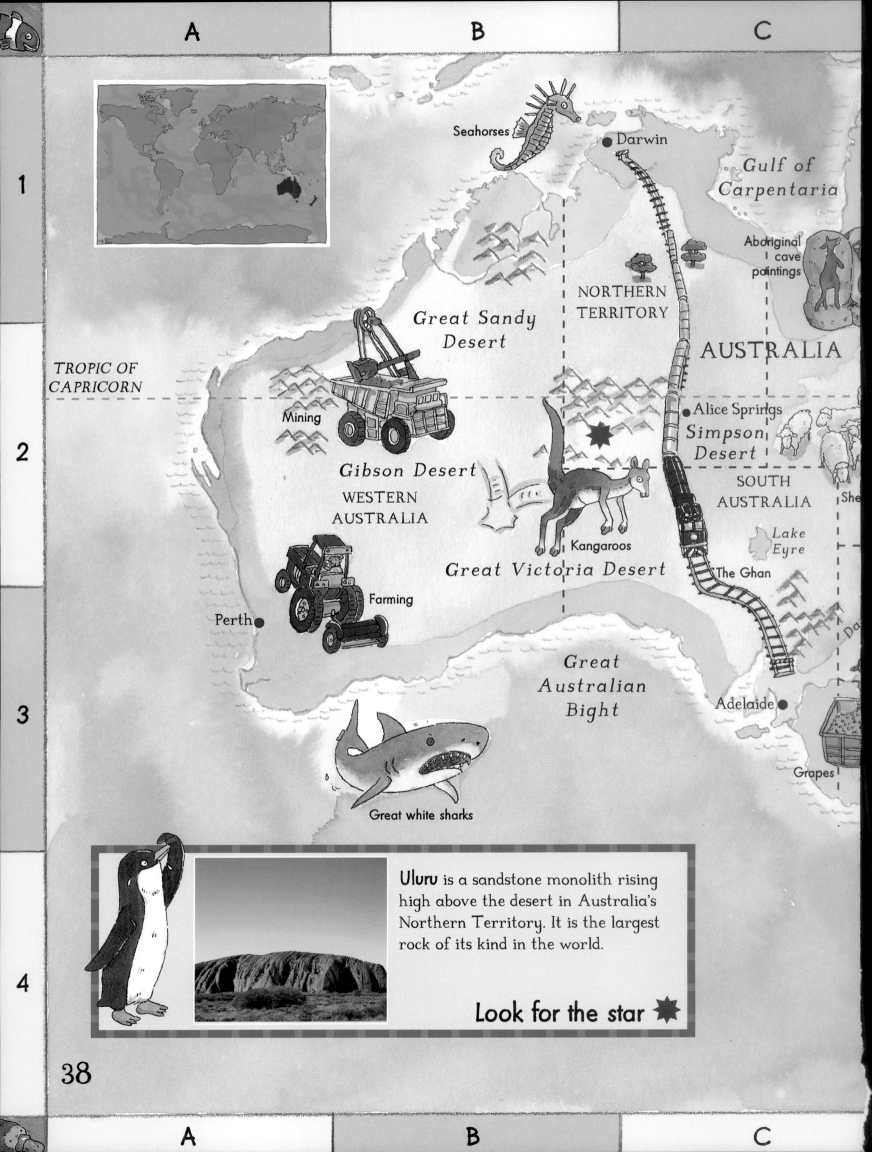

1

2

3

4

Seahorses

Darwin

Gulf of Carpentaria

Aboriginal cave paintings

NORTHERN TERRITORY

AUSTRALIA

Great Sandy Desert

Mining

TROPIC OF CAPRICORN

Gibson Desert

WESTERN AUSTRALIA

Farming

Perth

Alice Springs

Simpson Desert

SOUTH AUSTRALIA

Kangaroos

Great Victoria Desert

Lake Eyre

The Ghan

She

Great Australian Bight

Adelaide

Grapes

Great white sharks

Uluru is a sandstone monolith rising high above the desert in Australia's Northern Territory. It is the largest rock of its kind in the world.

Look for the star ✹

AUSTRALIA AND NEW ZEALAND

Australia is the only country that is also a continent. In the middle there are many deserts. To the north are tropical rain forests. Most Australian people live in cities by the sea. New Zealand is 620 miles from Australia. It is a land of mountains and glaciers. Like Australia, it has many sheep and cattle farms.

Great Barrier Reef

Coral Sea

Clown fish

Dividing Range

QUEENSLAND

Brisbane

x-billed platypuses

Pacific Ocean

NEW SOUTH WALES

Sydney Opera House

Sydney

Surfing

Canberra
AUSTRALIAN CAPITAL TERRITORY

urray

TORIA

bourne

ss Strait

Tasmanian devils

Tasman Sea

Hobart
TASMANIA

Red snapper fish

Rugby

NORTH ISLAND

NEW ZEALAND

Auckland

Hamilton

Lake Taupo

Kiwi birds

Wellington

SOUTH ISLAND

Southern Alps

Fishing

Mount Cook ▲

Christchurch

Dunedin

0   1000km

500 miles

Yellow-fin fish

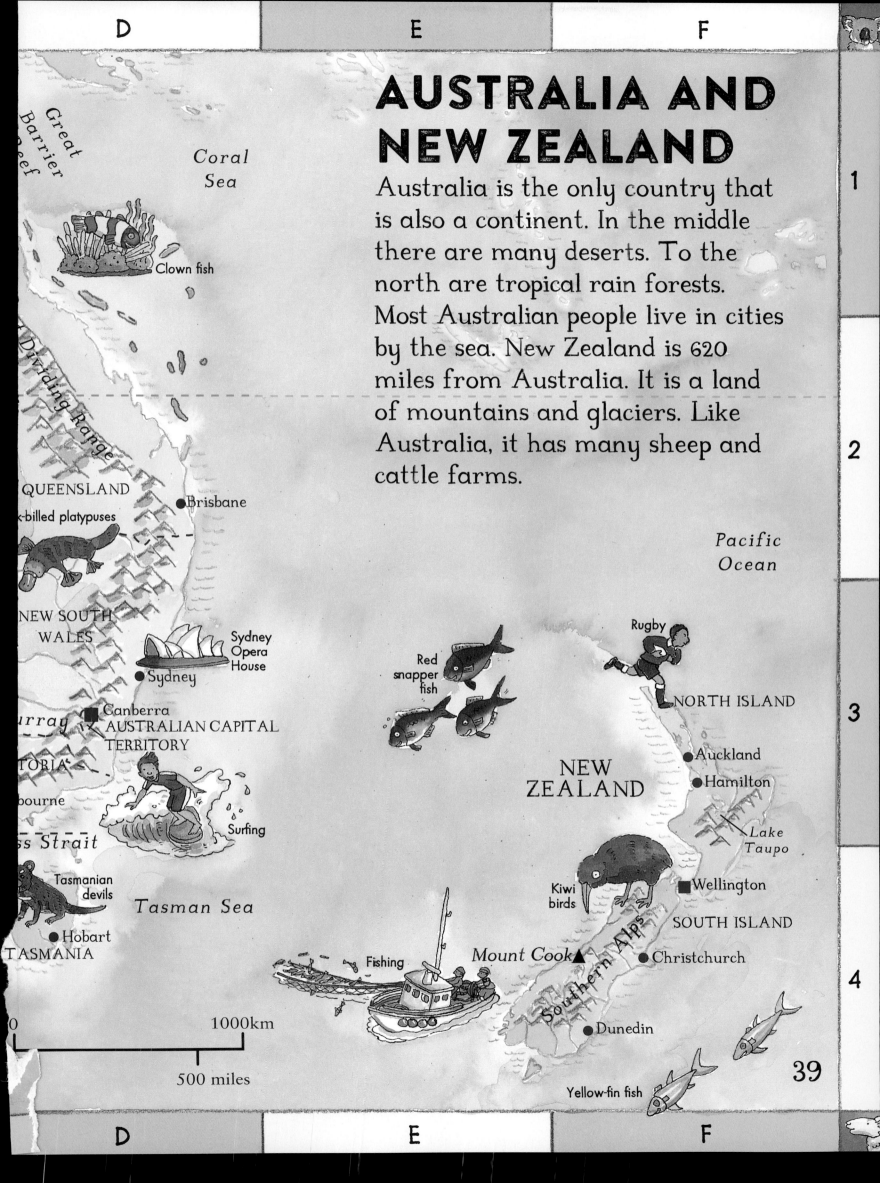

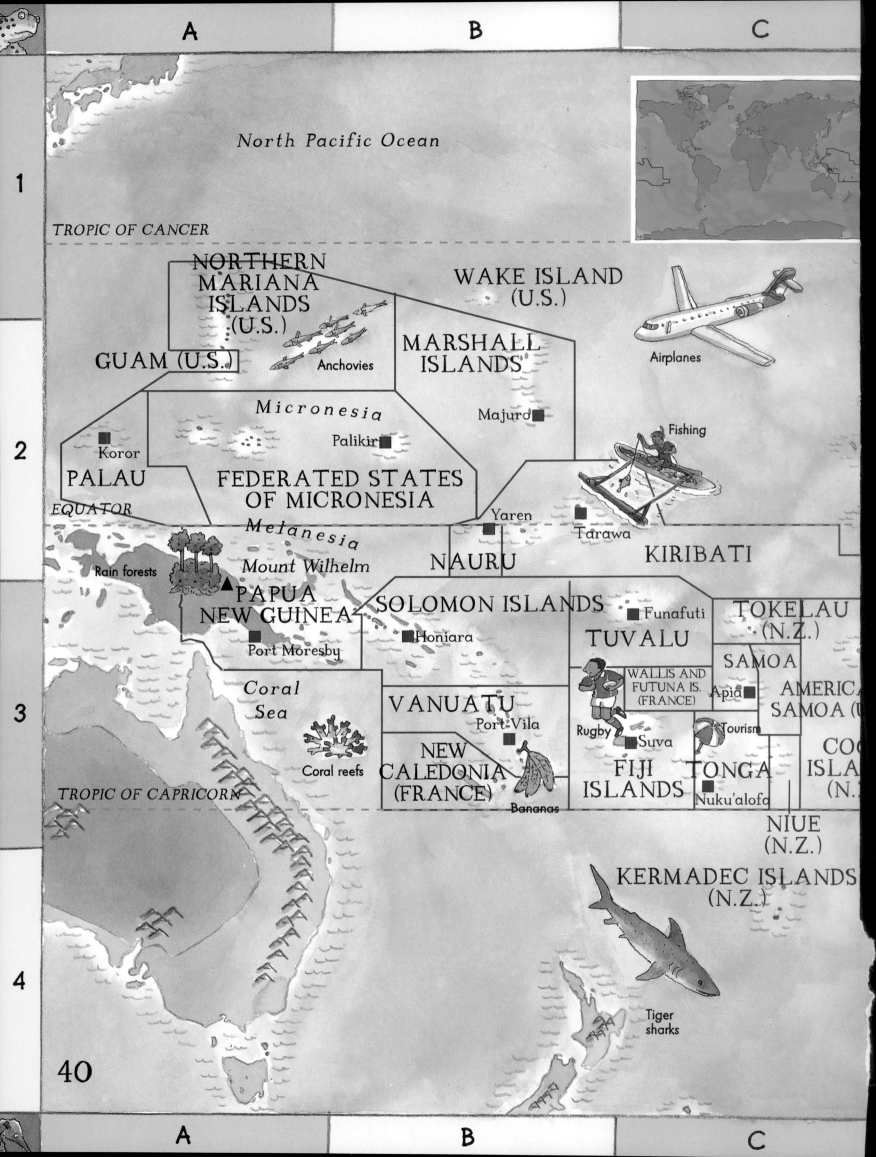

North Pacific Ocean

TROPIC OF CANCER

A **B** **C**

1

2

3

4

NORTHERN
MARIANA
ISLANDS
(U.S.)

WAKE ISLAND
(U.S.)

GUAM (U.S.)

Anchovies

MARSHALL
ISLANDS

Airplanes

Micronesia

Majuro

Koror

Palikir

Fishing

PALAU

FEDERATED STATES
OF MICRONESIA

EQUATOR

Melanesia

Yaren

Tarawa

KIRIBATI

Rain forests

Mount Wilhelm

NAURU

PAPUA
NEW GUINEA

SOLOMON ISLANDS

Funafuti

TOKELAU
(N.Z.)

Port Moresby

Honiara

TUVALU

SAMOA

Coral
Sea

VANUATU

WALLIS AND
FUTUNA IS.
(FRANCE)

Apia

AMERICA
SAMOA (

Coral reefs

NEW
CALEDONIA
(FRANCE)

Port-Vila

Rugby

Suva

FIJI
ISLANDS

Tourism

TONGA

COO
ISLA
(N.

TROPIC OF CAPRICORN

Bananas

Nuku'alofa

NIUE
(N.Z.)

KERMADEC ISLANDS
(N.Z.)

Tiger
sharks

A **B** **C**

THE PACIFIC ISLANDS

There are thousands of islands in the Pacific Ocean. All of these islands, with Australia, New Zealand, and Papua New Guinea, make up a region called Oceania. Many Pacific islanders live in communities that have little contact with the rest of the world. Some of their traditions have not changed for hundreds of years.

Over 1,000 years ago, settlers on Easter Island carved these huge **heads** out of volcanic rock. The statues may represent the island's great chiefs.

Look for the star ✹

Polynesia

Polynesian canoe
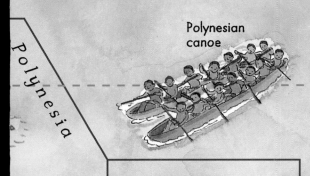

GALÁPAGOS ISLANDS
(ECUADOR)

Cruise ships

Sea turtles

FRENCH POLYNESIA
(FRANCE)

Long-nosed seahorses

PITCAIRN ISLANDS
(U.K.)

TROPIC OF CAPRICORN

✹ EASTER ISLAND
(CHILE)

South Pacific Ocean

0   1000km

0   500 miles

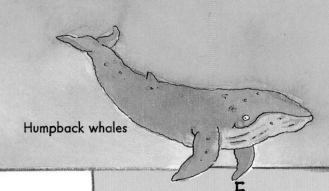
Humpback whales

41

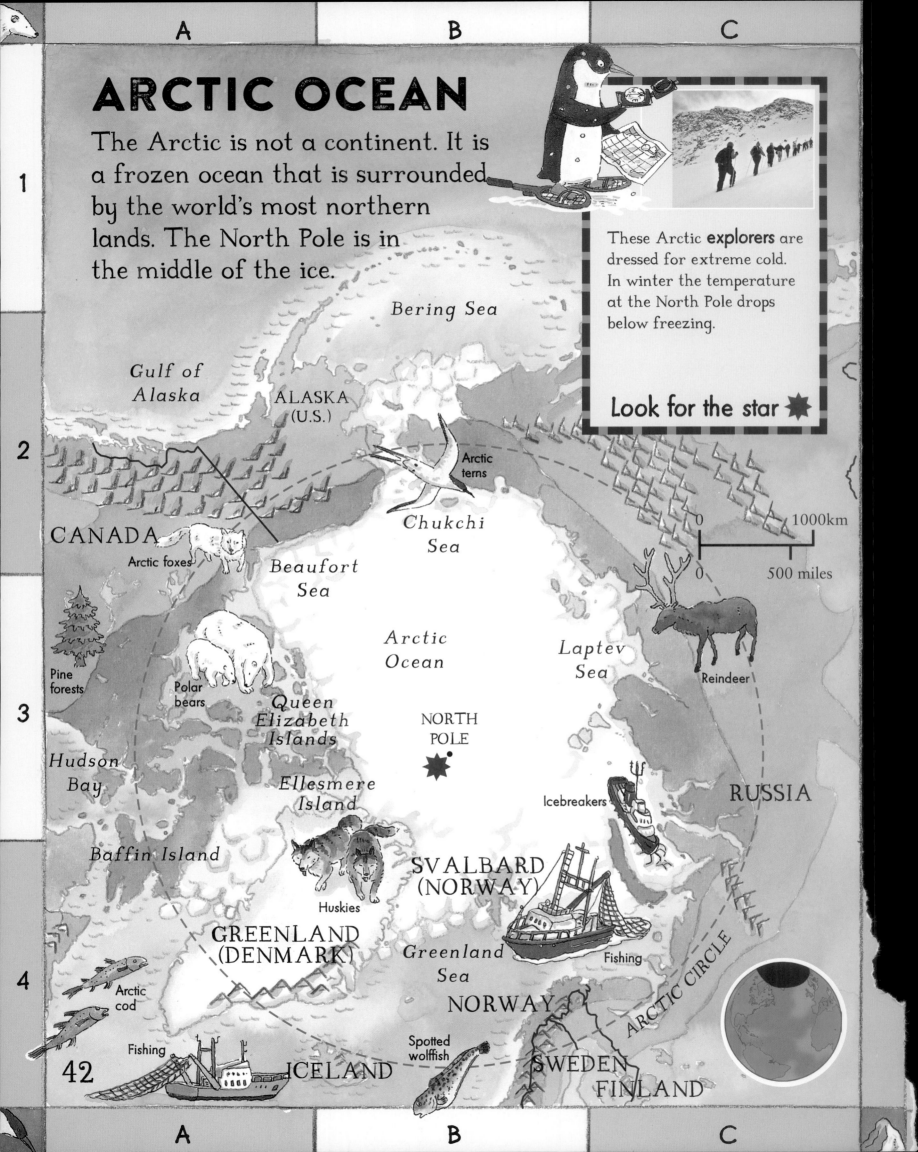

ARCTIC OCEAN

The Arctic is not a continent. It is a frozen ocean that is surrounded by the world's most northern lands. The North Pole is in the middle of the ice.

These Arctic **explorers** are dressed for extreme cold. In winter the temperature at the North Pole drops below freezing.

Look for the star ✴

Bering Sea

Gulf of Alaska

ALASKA (U.S.)

Arctic terns

Chukchi Sea

CANADA

Arctic foxes

Beaufort Sea

0   1000km

0   500 miles

Pine forests

Polar bears

Arctic Ocean

Laptev Sea

Reindeer

Queen Elizabeth Islands

NORTH POLE ✴ •

Hudson Bay

Ellesmere Island

Icebreakers

RUSSIA

Baffin Island

Huskies

SVALBARD (NORWAY)

GREENLAND (DENMARK)

Greenland Sea

Fishing

Arctic cod

NORWAY

ARCTIC CIRCLE

42

Fishing

Spotted wolffish

ICELAND

SWEDEN
FINLAND

ANTARCTICA

Antarctica is the world's most remote continent. Only scientists live here—in the coldest and windiest place on Earth. Almost all of Antarctica is covered with ice. The South Pole is in the middle of Antarctica.

0 — 1000km

0 — 500 miles

Antarctica has 90 percent of all the world's ice. The biggest **iceberg** spotted was found in the Antarctic and was bigger than the country of Belgium.

Look for the star ✴

Icebreakers

Atlantic Ocean

Icebergs

Antarctic Peninsula

Weddell Sea

Research stations

Indian Ocean

Leopard seals

Ronne Ice Shelf

▲ Vinson Massif

SOUTH POLE •

Greater Antarctica

King penguins

Lesser Antarctica

Amundsen Sea

Emperor penguins

Ross Ice Shelf

Pacific Ocean

Ross Sea

Explorers

Spiny icefish

4

Blue whales

Icebergs

ANTARCTIC CIRCLE

Warming's lantern fish

43

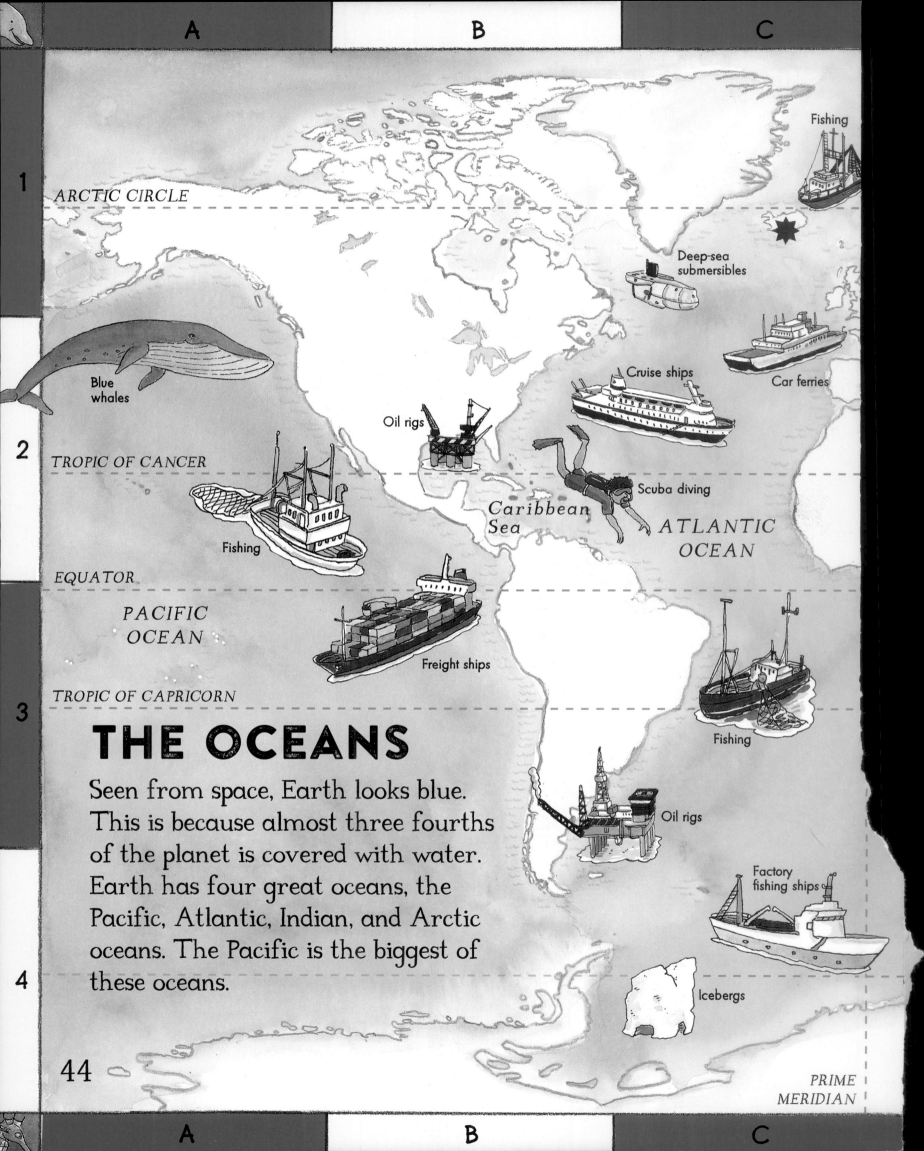

1

ARCTIC CIRCLE

Fishing

Deep-sea submersibles

Blue whales

Cruise ships

Car ferries

Oil rigs

2

TROPIC OF CANCER

Caribbean Sea

Scuba diving

ATLANTIC OCEAN

Fishing

EQUATOR

PACIFIC OCEAN

Freight ships

Fishing

TROPIC OF CAPRICORN

3

THE OCEANS

Seen from space, Earth looks blue.
This is because almost three fourths
of the planet is covered with water.
Earth has four great oceans, the
Pacific, Atlantic, Indian, and Arctic
oceans. The Pacific is the biggest of
these oceans.

Oil rigs

Factory fishing ships

4

Icebergs

PRIME MERIDIAN

Icebreakers

ARCTIC OCEAN

1

Submarines

Luxury yachts

PACIFIC OCEAN

Chinese junks

2

Arabian Sea

Bay of Bengal

Fishing

INDIAN OCEAN

Oil tankers

Coral Sea

Coral reefs

Airplanes

3

Oil rigs

Racing yachts

ANTARCTIC CIRCLE

Many **islands** are actually the peaks of underwater mountains. Iceland is the tip of one of the mountains of the Mid-Atlantic Ridge.

Look for the star ✸

4

Index

ood Hope, Cape of *headland* 37 B6
öteborg Sweden 21 D4
otland *island* 21 E4
rande, Rio *river* 16 B2
reat European Plain *physical region* 24 A1
reece *country* 25 C5
reat Australian Bight *bay* 38 B3
reat Barrier Reef *reef* 39 D1
reat Bear Lake *lake* 12 C2
reat Dividing Range *mountains* 39 D1
reat Indian Desert *desert* 30 A1
reat Rift Valley *valley* 36 C2
reat Salt Lake *lake* 14 C2
reat Sandy Desert *desert* 38 B2
reat Slave Lake *lake* 12 C3
reat Victoria Desert *desert* 38 B2
reater Antarctica *physical region* 43 B3
eenland Danish *dependent territory* 42 A4
reenland Sea *sea* 42 B4
renada *country* 17 F4
uam US *dependent territory* 40 A2
uangzhou China 33 D4
uatemala *country* 16 C3
uatemala City Guatemala 16 C3
uiana Highlands *physical region* 18 B1
uinea *country* 34 A3
uinea-Bissau *country* 34 A3
ulf, The *gulf* 29 D3
uyana *country* 18 B1

H
Hainan *island* 32 C4
aiti *country* 17 D3
amilton New Zealand 39 F3
ammerfest Norway 21 E1
anoi Vietnam 31 D2
arare Zimbabwe 37 C4
arbin China 33 E2
avana Cuba 17 D2
awaii *state* U.S. 14 A2
Helsinki Finland 21 F3
malayas *mountains* 30 B1, 32 A3
bart Australia 39 D4
kkaido *island* 33 F2
nduras *country* 17 D3
ng Kong China 33 D4
niara Solomon Islands 40 B3
nshu *island* 33 F2
rn, Cape *headland* 19 B6
uston Texas, U.S. 15 D4
uang He *river* 32 C2
dson Bay *bay* 13 E3, 42 A3
ungary *country* 24 B3
Huron, Lake *lake* 13 E4, 15 E2

IJ
Iceland *country* 20 A1, 42 B4
Idaho *state* U.S. 14 B2
Illinois *state* U.S. 15 E2
India *country* 30 B2
Indian Ocean *ocean* 30 A4, 35 F4, 43 C2, 45 D3
Indiana *state* U.S. 15 E2
Indonesia *country* 31 D4
Indus *river* 30 A1
Iowa *state* U.S. 15 D2
Iran *country* 29 E2
Iraq *country* 29 D2
Ireland *country* 22 A3

Islamabad r... an 30 A1
Israel *country* 28 C2
Istanbul Turkey 28 B1
Italy *country* 23 D6
Ivory Coast *country* 34 A3
Izmir Turkey 28 B1
Jakarta Indonesia 31 D4
Jamaica *country* 17 D3
Japan *country* 33 F3
Japan, Sea of *sea* 33 E2
Jerusalem Israel 28 C2
Jordan *country* 28 C2
Juba South Sudan 35 D3

K
Kabul Afghanistan 30 A1
Kalahari Desert *desert* 37 B5
Kamchatka Peninsula *geographical region* 27 E3
Kampala Uganda 36 C3
Kansas *state* U.S. 15 D5
Karachi Pakistan 30 A2
Kathmandu Nepal 30 B1
Kazakhstan *country* 26 B4
Kazanlak Bulgaria 25 C4
Kentucky *state* U.S. 15 E3
Kenya *country* 36 C2
Kermadec Islands N.Z. dependent territory 40 C4
Khartoum Sudan 35 E2
Kiev Ukraine 26 A4
Kigali Rwanda 36 C3
Kilimanjaro, Mount *mountain* 36 C3
Kingston Jamaica 17 D3
Kinshasa Democratic Republic of Congo 36 A3
Kiribati *country* 40 C2
Kiruna Sweden 21 E2
Kolkata India 30 B2
Koror Palau 40 A2
Kosovo *country* 25 C4
Krakow Poland 24 B2
Kuala Lumpur Malaysia 30 C3
Kuwait *country* 29 D2
Kuwait City Kuwait 29 D2
Kyrgyzstan *country* 26 B4
Kyushu *island* 33 E3

L
La Paz Bolivia 18 B3
Laâyoune Western Sahara 34 A2
Lake region *geographical region* 21 F3
Laos *country* 31 D2
Lapland *geographical region* 21 E1
Latvia *country* 21 E4
Lebanon *country* 28 C2
Lena *river* 27 D2
Lesotho *country* 37 C5
Lesser Antarctica *physical region* 43 B3
Lhasa China 32 B3
Liberia *country* 34 A3
Libreville Gabon 36 A3
Libya *country* 34 C2
Liechtenstein *country* 23 C4
Lilongwe Malawi 37 C4
Lima Peru 18 A2
Limpopo *river* 37 C4
Lisbon Portugal 23 A6
Lithuania *country* 21 E4
Ljubljana Slovenia 24 A3

Loire *river* 23 B4
Lomé Togo 34 B4
London United Kingdom 23 B4
Los Angeles California, U.S. 14 B3
Louisiana *state* U.S. 15 D3
Luanda Angola 36 A3
Lusaka Zambia 37 C4
Luxembourg *country* 23 C4
Luxembourg Luxembourg 23 C4
Lyon France 23 C5

M
Mackenzie *river* 12 C2
Madagascar *country* 37 D4
Madrid Spain 23 B6
Maine *state* U.S. 15 F2
Majuro Marshall Islands 40 B2
Malabo Equatorial Guinea 36 A2
Malawi *country* 37 C4
Malawi, Lake *lake* 37 C4
Malaysia *country* 31 D3
Maldives *country* 30 A3
Male Maldives 30 A3
Mali *country* 34 B3
Malta *country* 23 D6
Managua Nicaragua 16 C4
Manama Bahrain 29 D3
Manila Philippines 31 D3
Manitoba *province* Canada 13 D3
Maputo Mozambique 37 C5
Maracaibo, Lake *lake* 18 A1
Marseille France 23 C5
Marshall Islands *country* 40 B2
Maryland *state* U.S. 15 F3
Maseru Lesotho 37 B5
Mashhad Iran 29 E1
Massachusetts *state* U.S. 15 F2
Mauritania *country* 34 A2
Mbabane Swaziland 37 C5
McKinley, Mount *mountain* 12 B3
Mecca Saudi Arabia 28 C3
Medina Saudi Arabia 28 C3
Mediterranean Sea *sea* 23 C6, 25 C6, 28 A2, 34 C1, 45 D2
Mekong *river* 31 D2
Melanesia *region* 40 A2
Melbourne Australia 39 D3
Mexico *country* 16 B2
Mexico City Mexico 16 B3
Mexico, Gulf of *gulf* 15 D4, 16 C2
Miami U.S. 15 E4
Michigan, Lake *lake* 15 E2
Michigan *state* U.S. 15 E2
Micronesia *region* 40 A2
Minnesota *state* U.S. 15 D2
Minsk Belarus 26 A3
Mississippi *river* 15 E3
Mississippi *state* U.S. 15 E3
Missouri *river* 15 D2
Missouri *state* U.S. 15 D3
Mogadishu Somalia 35 F4
Moldova *country* 26 A4
Monaco *country* 23 C5
Mongolia *country* 32 B1
Monrovia Liberia 34 A3
Montana *state* U.S. 14 C2
Montenegro *country* 25 B4
Montevideo Uruguay 19 C4
Montreal Canada 13 E4
Morocco *country* 34 A1
Moroni Comoros 37 D4

Moscow Russia 26 A3
Mosul Iraq 29 D1
Mozambique *country* 37 C5
Mumbai (Bombay) India 30 A2
Munich Germany 23 D4
Murmansk Russia 26 A2
Murray *river* 39 D3
Muscat Oman 29 E3

N
Nagoya Japan 33 E3
Nairobi Kenya 36 C3
Namib Desert *desert* 37 A5
Namibia *country* 37 A4
Nassau Bahamas 17 D2
Nasser, Lake *lake* 35 D2
Nauru *country* 40 B2
N'Djamena Chad 34 C3
Nepal *country* 30 B1
Netherlands *country* 22 B3
Nebraska *state* U.S. 15 D2
Nevada *state* U.S. 15 B2
New Brunswick *province* Canada 13 F4
New Caledonia *French dependent territory* 40 B3
New Guinea *country* 40 A3
New Hampshire *state* U.S. 15 F2
New Jersey *state* U.S. 15 F2
New Mexico *state* U.S. 14 C3
New Orleans Louisiana, U.S. 15 E4
New Siberian Islands *islands* 27 E1
New South Wales *state* Australia 39 D3
New Zealand (N.Z.) *country* 39 F3
New York *state* U.S. 15 F2
New York City U.S. 15 F2
Newfoundland and Labrador *province* Canada 13 F4
Niamey Niger 34 B3
Nicaragua *country* 17 D3
Nicosia Cyprus 28 C2
Niger *country* 34 C3
Niger *river* 34 B3
Nigeria *country* 34 C3
Nile *river* 35 E2
Niue *N.Z. dependent territory* 40 C3
Nizhny Novgorod Russia 26 A3
North America *continent* 10 B2
North Carolina *state* U.S. 15 E3
North Dakota *state* U.S. 15 D1
North Korea *country* 33 E2
North Island *island* 39 F3
North Macedonia *country* 25 C5
North Pole *pole* 42 B3
North Sea *sea* 20 C4, 22 B3
Northern Ireland *national region* U.K. 22 A3
Northern Mariana Islands *U.S. dependent territory* 40 A1
Northern Territory *state* Australia 38 B1
Northwest Territories *territory* Canada 12 C3
Norway *country* 21 D3, 42 B4
Norwegian Sea *sea* 21 D2
Nouakchott Mauritania 34 A3
Nova Scotia *province* Canada 13 F4
Novaya Zemlya *islands* 26 B2
Novosibirsk Russia 26 C3
Nuku'alofa Tonga 40 C3
Nunavut *territory* Canada 13 E2
Nur-Sultan Kazakhstan 26 B4

47

OP

Ob *river* 26 B3
Oder *river* 24 B2
Ohio *state* U.S. 15 E2
Okhotsk, Sea of *sea* 27 E4
Oklahoma *state* U.S. 15 D3
Oman *country* 29 E3
Omsk Russia 26 B3
Ontario, Lake *lake* 13 E4, 15 F2
Ontario *province* Canada 13 E4
Orange *river* 37 B5
Oregon *state* U.S. 14 B2
Osaka Japan 33 E3
Oslo Norway 21 D3
Ottawa Canada 13 E4
Ouagadougou Burkina Faso 34 B3
Oulu Finland 21 F2
Oulujärvi *lake* 21 F2
Pacific Ocean *ocean* 12 B4, 14 A2, 16 A3, 18
A3, 27 F4, 39 F2, 40–41, 43 A4,
44 A3, 45 F2
Pakistan *country* 30 A1
Palau *country* 40 A2
Palikir Federated States of Micronesia 40 B2
Panama *country* 17 D4
Panama City Panama 17 D4
Paraguay *country* 18 B3
Paramaribo Surinam 18 C1
Paraná *river* 19 B4
Paris France 23 B4
Patagonia *physical region* 19 B5
Pennsylvania *state* U.S. 15 E2
Perth Australia 38 A3
Peru *country* 18 A2
Philadelphia Pennsylvania, U.S. 15 F2
Philippines *country* 31 D3
Phnom Pen Cambodia 31 D3
Pitcairn Islands *U.K. dependent territory* 41 E3
Plateau of Tibet *plateau* 32 A3
Po *river* 23 C5
Podgorica Montenegro 25 B4
Poland *country* 24 B1
Polynesia *region* 41 D2, D3
Port Moresby Papua New Guinea 40 A3
Port-au-Prince Haiti 17 E3
Port-of-Spain Trinidad & Tobago 17 F4
Porto Novo Benin 34 B4
Portugal *country* 23 A6
Port-Vila Vanuatu 40 B3
Prague Czech Republic 24 A2
Prince Edward Island *province* Canada 13 F4
Pristina Kosovo 25 C4
Puerto Rico *U.S. dependent territory* 17 E3
Pyongyang North Korea 33 E2
Pyrenees *mountains* 23 B5

QR

Qatar *country* 29 D3
Québec Canada 13 E4
Québec *province* Canada 13 E4
Queen Elizabeth Islands *islands* 13 D1, 42 A3
Queensland *state* Australia 39 D2
Quito Ecuador 18 A1
Rabat Morocco 34 A1
Rangoon Burma (Myanmar) 30 C2
Red Sea *sea* 28 C3, 35 E2
Rhode Island *state* U.S. 15 F2
Rio de Janeiro Brazil 18 C3
Riyadh Saudi Arabia 29 D3
Reykjavik Iceland 20 A2
Rhodes *island* 25 D6

Rhône *river* 23 C5
Ríga Latvia 21 E4
Rocky Mountains *mountains* 12 C3, 14 B2
Romania *country* 24 C3
Rome Italy 23 D5
Ronne Ice Shelf *ice shelf* 43 A3
Ross Ice Shelf *ice shelf* 43 B4
Ross Sea *sea* 43 B4
Russia *country* 26 C3, 42 C3
Rwanda *country* 36 C3

S

Sahara *desert* 34 B2
St Kitts & Nevis *country* 17 E3
St Lawrence *river* 13 F4
St Lucia *country* 17 F3
St Petersburg Russia 26 A3
St Vincent & the Grenadines *country* 17 F3
Salvador Brazil 18 D2
Samara Russia 26 B4
Samoa *country* 40 C3
San Antonio U.S. 15 D4
San Diego U.S. 14 B3
San Francisco U.S. 14 B3
San José Costa Rica 17 D4
San Juan Puerto Rico 17 E3
San Marino *country* 23 D5
San Salvador El Salvador 16 C3
Sana Yemen 29 D4
Santa Fé Argentina 19 B4
Santiago Chile 19 B4
Santo Domingo Dominican Republic 17 E3
São Paulo Brazil 18 C3
São Tomé São Tomé and Príncipe 36 A3
São Tomé and Príncipe *country* 36 A3
Sarajevo Bosnia and Herzogovina 25 B4
Sardinia *island* 23 C5
Saskatchewan *province* Canada 13 D4
Saudi Arabia *country* 29 D3
Scotland *national region* U.K. 22 A3
Seattle U.S. 14 B1
Seine *river* 23 B4
Senegal *country* 34 A3
Seoul South Korea 33 E3
Serbia *country* 25 B4
Severnaya Zemlya *islands* 26 C1
Seychelles *country* 36 D1
Shanghai China 33 D3
Shenyang China 33 D2
Shikoku *island* 33 E3
Siberia *physical region* 26 C2
Sicily *island* 23 D6
Sierra Leone *country* 34 A3
Simpson Desert *desert* 38 C2
Singapore *country* 31 D4
Singapore Singapore 31 D4
Skopje Macedonia 25 C4
Slovakia *country* 24 B3
Slovenia *country* 24 A3
Sofia Bulgaria 25 C4
Solomon Islands *country* 40 B3
Somalia *country* 35 E4
South Africa *country* 37 B5
South America *continent* 10 B3
South Australia *state* Australia 38 C2
South Carolina *state* U.S. 15 E3
South China Sea *sea* 31 D2, 33 D4
South Dakota *state* U.S. 15 D2
South Island *island* 39 F4
South Korea *country* 33 E3
South Pole *pole* 43 B3
South Sudan *country* 35 D3

Southern Alps *mountains* 39 F4
Spain *country* 23 B6
Sri Lanka *country* 30 B3
Stanley Falkland Islands 19 C5
Stockholm Sweden 21 E3
Sudan *country* 35 D3
Superior, Lake *lake* 13 E4, 15 E1
Surinam *country* 18 B1
Suva Fiji 40 C3
Svalbard *Norwegian dependent territory* 42
B4
Sweden *country* 21 E2, 42 B4
Switzerland *country* 23 C5
Sydney Australia 39 D3
Syria *country* 28 C2

T

Tabriz Iran 29 D1
Taipei Taiwan 33 D4
Taiwan *country* 33 D4
Tajikistan *country* 26 B4
Taklimakan Desert *desert* 32 B2
Tallinn Estonia 21 F3
Tanganyika, Lake *lake* 36 C3
Tanzania *country* 36 C3
Tarawa Kiribati 40 B2
Tashkent Uzbekistan 26 B4
Tasman Sea *sea* 39 D4
Tasmania *state* Australia 39 D4
Taupo, Lake *lake* 39 F3
Taymyr Peninsula *geographical region*
27 D1
Tbilisi Georgia 26 A4
Tegucigalpa Honduras 16 C3
Tehran Iran 29 D1
Tennessee *state* U.S. 15 E3
Texas *state* U.S. 15 D3
Thailand *country* 30 C2
Thessaloníki Greece 25 C5
Thimpu Bhutan 30 C1
Tianjin China 33 D2
Tibesti Mountains *mountains* 34 C2
Tigris *river* 29 D2
Tirana Albania 25 B5
Titicaca, Lake *lake* 18 A2
Togo *country* 34 B3
Tokelau *N.Z. dependent territory* 40 C3
Tokyo Japan 33 F3
Tonga *country* 40 C3
Transylvanian Alps *mountains* 25 C4
Trinidad & Tobago *country* 17 F4
Tripoli Libya 34 C1
Trondheim Norway 21 D3
Tshwane (Pretoria) South Africa 37 B5
Tunis Tunisia 34 C1
Tunisia *country* 34 C1
Turkey *country* 28 B1
Turkmenistan *country* 26 B4
Tuvalu *country* 40 C3

U

Uganda *country* 36 C2
Ukraine *country* 26 A4
Ulan Bator Mongolia 32 C1
United Arab Emirates (U.A.E.) *country* 29 E3
United Kingdom (U.K.) *country* 22 B3
United States of America (U.S.) *country*
14–15
Ural *river* 26 B4
Ural Mountains *mountains* 26 B3
Uruguay *country* 19 C4

Urümqi China 32 B2
Utah *state* U.S. 14 C2
Uzbekistan *country* 26 B4

V

Vaduz Liechtenstein 23 C4
Valletta Malta 23 D6
Van, Lake *lake* 29 D1
Vancouver Canada 12 C4
Vanuatu *country* 40 B3
Vättern *lake* 21 E4
Venezuela *country* 18 B1
Vermont *state* U.S. 15 F2
Victoria, Lake *lake* 36 C3
Victoria Seychelles 36 D1
Victoria *state* Australia 39 D3
Victoria Island *island* 13 D2
Vienna Austria 23 D4
Vientiane Laos 30 C2
Vietnam *country* 31 D2
Vilnius Lithuania 21 F4
Vinson Massif *mountain* 43 A3
Virginia *state* U.S. 15 E3
Vistula *river* 24 B1
Vladivostok Russia 27 D4
Volga *river* 26 A4

W

Wales *national region* U.K. 22 A3
Wake Island *U.S. dependent territory* 40 B1
Wallis and Futuna Islands *French dependent*
territory 40 C3
Warsaw Poland 24 C1
Washington *state* U.S. 14 B1
Washington D.C. (District of Columbia) U.S.
15 F3
Weddell Sea *sea* 43 A3
Wellington New Zealand 39 F4
West Sierra Madre *mountains* 16 A2
West Virginia *state* U.S. 15 E2
Western Australia *state* Australia 38 B2
Western Sahara *disputed region* 34 A2
Wilhelm, Mount *mountain* 40 A2
Windhoek Namibia 37 B4
Winnipeg, Lake *lake* 13 D4
Wisconsin *state* U.S. 15 D2
Wuhan China 33 D3
Wyoming *state* U.S. 14 C2

XY

Xian China 32 C3
Yakutsk Russia 27 D3
Yamoussoukro Ivory Coast 34 B4
Yaoundé Cameroon 36 A2
Yaren Nauru 40 B2
Yekaterinburg Russia 26 B3
Yemen *country* 29 D4
Yenisey *river* 26 C3
Yerevan Armenia 26 A4
Yucatán Peninsula *peninsula* 16 C3
Yukon *river* 12 B2
Yukon Territory *territory* Canada 12 B3

Z

Zagreb Croatia 24 A3
Zagros Mountains *mountains* 29 D2
Zambezi *river* 37 C4
Zambia *country* 37 B4
Zimbabwe *country* 37 C4